Ask the Animals

Ask the Animals

Life Lessons Learned as an Animal Communicator

Kim Ogden-Avrutik, Dr.P.H.

Lantern Books • New York
A Division of Booklight Inc.

2003

Lantern Books

One Union Square West, Suite 201

New York, NY 10003

Printed in Canada

Except where clients have asked that real names be used, the human and animal
names in this book have been changed. Unless otherwise stated, the photos in this
book depict the actual animals featured in the stories. None of the information in
this book is intended to replace the advice of your veterinarian.

Cover photo by Studio West
Cover photo enhancement by Rikki Poulos
Photos of Chuma (page 3) and Catelda (page 15) by Robert Chesrow
Photo of Stanley (page 7) by Kate Murphy
Photo of Misty (page 69) by Louisa Emerick
Photos of Tai Tai (pages 89 and 137) by Tom Avrutik

Library of Congress Cataloging-in-Publication Data

Ogden-Avrutik, Kim.
Ask the animals : life lessons learned as an animal communicator /Kim Ogden-
Avrutik.
p. cm. ISBN 1-59056-046-9 (alk. paper)
1. Pets—Behavior—Anecdotes. 2. Domestic animals—Behavior—Anecdotes. 3.
Human-animal communication—Anecdotes. 4. Ogden-Avrutik, Kim. 5. Animal
communicators—Anecdotes. I. Title.
SF412.5.O35 2003
636.088'7—dc21
2003005256

printed on 100% post-consumer waste paper, chlorine-free

The God of the whole gave a living soul
To furred and to feathered thing.
And I am my brother's keeper.
And I will fight his fight;
And speak for the beast and bird
Till the world shall set things right.

Ella Wheeler Wilcox

Acknowledgments

~

MY HEARTFELT THANKS GO FIRST TO THE GREAT SPIRIT for giving me opportunities to assist others on their spiritual path. This includes both animals and humans. Intuition, love and focus are just three of the wonderful qualities you have provided to us all. As such, we can surely talk to each other—and to you. Thank you.

To all who have helped our animal friends to be treated respectfully or have mapped a path before me in this work. This includes family, friends, clients and people I've never even met. To Sarah Gallogly, who embraced the potential for this book to help our animal friends and did such fine editing.

A special "thank you" goes to my husband, Tom, for putting up with me through all the years of my whining and complaining about not really knowing what I wanted to do or what made me feel good. Now I know. Thank you for your patience, love and trust.

And to all the animals. Thank you for loving us humans, and for loving us despite our faults. Thank you for teaching us new ways to look at you, ourselves, the universe and God.

Contents

Preface

PEOPLE ALWAYS ASK ME HOW I BECAME AN ANIMAL COMmunicator. That story in itself could almost make another book. Even though I loved animals as a child and often "felt" what they felt, I didn't recognize this intuitive gift. Feeling that others knew better than I did, I got proficient in careers that focused on the sciences: I was a Registered Dietitian, I received a master's and a doctorate in public health. I tried this and that, and to the outside world I appeared successful. But I was never totally happy with what I did.

When I took the first steps on the road to this profession, I had worked in the field of public health for more than fifteen years. I had no other plans beyond continuing to work with the "underdog"—the low-income, often poorly educated group that public health professionals can influence. My life took a strange turn, however, when my husband and I moved temporarily to Taiwan, Republic of China, on business. I saw this as a unique opportunity to learn about the Chinese culture and public health concerns. What I saw, first hand, changed my life forever. I saw extreme poverty and abuse—not in the human population, but in the animal population. In the early 1990s Taiwan did not have an active animal humane society, nor did the international community comprehend what was happening to the animals on the streets.

After coming to the realization that many of the same abuses I saw in Taiwan still confronted animals in the United States, I decided to make some life changes. I decided that what I really wanted to do was to serve a new population—the animal population. I reasoned that if I could increase the general public's respect for animals, the abuse would decrease. But how would I do this?

When I asked the Great Spirit for direction, all I heard was "Be happy," or "It's right out your back door." Little did I know that my happiness was, indeed, right out my back door, where scores of wild animals gathered—raccoons, mice, beavers, a fox. These were visitors to our yard in northern Illinois.

One day in my house, desperate to know what I should do professionally, I remember shouting at the top of my voice, saying "If I could do one thing before I leave this earth, I want to be able to talk with animals."

In hindsight, it's clear now that I didn't recognize my old gift. I had forgotten, with all that logical training in the sciences, that my intuitive abilities were, at least at one time, very high. As a young girl, I could "feel" what the animals felt, but I didn't recognize this as being able to communicate with them. Yet even in my "unawareness," I knew when there was an animal in trouble in the back yard, and sure enough, an animal would come limping in that night.

So all I had to do was remember. "Remembering" came soon after the day we rescued Boxie, an eight-year-old Cocker Spaniel who had not been kept in the best of conditions. He had never been housetrained, he barked all night long and he chased our four cats. Then I remembered reading somewhere about animal communication. I went on the Web. I read books. I realized I had been doing many of the things an animal communicator does. But I was as skeptical as the next person, and Boxie wasn't much of a talker. I still didn't believe in my own abilities.

Eventually, I contacted a professional animal communicator for help with Boxie. I was impressed by the valuable insights he was able to provide in just that one session. But he also told me something that was on my female cat's mind—something she'd told me herself that very morning!

Bingo! I started jumping around the house. "I can really do this!" I thought. Then I got scared—"Uh oh . . . I can really do this!" Ultimately, I realized my pleas to a Higher Power had been answered: I had finally found my path. I guess all I needed was verification.

I practiced my own accelerated animal communication course. I practiced with the cats, with Boxie, with birds, deer, squirrels, any non-human creature who would communicate with me. I practiced morning, noon and evening; then I practiced with night animals. At two or three in the morning I found myself practicing with owls or raccoons. And within about three weeks, Boxie was housetrained. He stopped barking at night, and he has never chased any of the cats again. I kept practicing, and within a short time, I had my first official case. I've been busy ever since. All I needed was confidence. I had learned a lifetime's worth of lessons from the animals, and they were very good teachers.

I love being an animal communicator. It fits me. Helping to solve problems and aiding the understanding between animals and humans makes me feel alive. All the cases I work on are fascinating. Most give insights into the human client, and all teach me lessons. Lessons that show that the creatures we call "animals" are sentient, loving, kind beings with limitless compassion for their humans. Lessons that show me more about human thought and how it can be elevated. Lessons that show that animals want the same things we want: food, shelter, love, respect and kindness. I also have had cases of animals who wanted to learn more about a Higher Power. It has been my pleasure to share what I know with them, and in turn to gain their friendship and the joy of having made a difference in their lives.

The thing that satisfies me most, however, is sharing what I have learned about these spiritual creatures we call animals. From my experience, I have come to recognize these creatures as spiritual lesson-givers that a knowing Force puts in our path. It's clear to me it's no accident that we have chosen certain animals or that they have chosen us. In my belief system, Spirit puts them there so we can grow faster from the lessons they teach us.

When I see my four cats itching in unison, I know they don't have fleas. I have taken precautions so they don't. I have come to recognize that their irritation is really my irritation. I immediately take a few minutes to check in and see if I am feeling irritated about something. If something comes to mind, I tackle it as best as I can. I get calm, and I bring myself into harmony. Then I look around and sure enough, not one cat is itching any more. The change is marvelous to behold.

There is a golden thread of information among animal communicators on "how to" contact and communicate with an animal. This, however, is not a how-to book. Instead, it's mainly about seeing animals as lesson-giving "gifts"—intelligent friends who gently prompt us to face our own issues. In this sense, and in the love they give us and inspire in our hearts, animals are loving gifts from God.

People ask me all the time what my work as an animal communicator has to do with my training in public health. The answer is "everything!" I feel that animals are part of the public, too, and as such, deserve love, respect and quality care. Just as in public health, the "care" aspect can be sad. Sometimes I wish I had never heard what an animal said, especially if he or she told me about days, months or years of abuse with a former "owner."

I continue, however, because I feel the work is making a difference. Often I am the animals' and the humans' last resort. People come to me in desperation about their animals' health, habits or peculiarities. Although I can't provide a medical diagnosis, I can relate what an animal friend communicates about a particular discomfort he or she is experiencing, which is often helpful in getting an animal appropriate veterinary care. Other times, the discomfort is emotional. Every species that has communicated with me experiences joys and sadness in much the same way that humans do—not just animals who purr or lick our faces to show their delight, but also our scaled and swimming friends, whose capacity for feeling is so often underestimated.

My goal is to heighten people's awareness of their animals' intelligence, sentience and compassion by letting people know how their animals think and feel, sharing the animals' words and feelings as directly as I can. In case after case, I have seen that the information provided in a consultation increases people's love and respect for their animal friends. It also joyfully increases the animal friends' understanding of their humans. In communicating with an animal, a process begins with both animal and human cooperating, attempting to salvage a relationship that has often become difficult for both. Hearts are opened, and a more positive relationship begins to form. This book is filled with such stories, and I hope you enjoy reading it.

Why *Ask the Animals* Was Written

I am in favor of animal rights as well as human rights. This is the way of the whole human being.

Abraham Lincoln

I WROTE THIS BOOK IN ORDER TO SHARE A BODY OF EXPERIENCE with you. The stories in this book, based on actual case studies, show that animals are sentient, intelligent beings who can share their thoughts and feelings and help us grow spiritually. My hope is that *Ask the Animals* will further increase your awareness about the high caliber of consciousness that animals have. Each of the short stories presents a situation and shares the thoughts and emotions of both human and animal companion. You can see the process that goes on between the animal and his or her guardian in order to achieve a relationship that works for both.

Whether you live with an animal friend or not, you will begin to see animals as companions with whom you can share your deepest fears and joys. When you first begin to realize this, especially when you can see it in your own animal friend, something wonderful happens. Your first reaction may be surprise: it's as if you just discovered that a dear old friend has a majestic heritage. Some people cry for joy. Perhaps it's because they always knew deep inside that their loving animal friend had more to tell them than they understood. It is rare for me to meet a person who doesn't want to know more about what their animal friend has to say to them.

It is a dream come true for me to be of service to a human and animal public that has the ability to share friendship, thoughts and feelings with each other. My work is rewarding every day—because if there's one thing I've learned from thousands of two-legged, four-legged, water-dwelling, crawling and winged beings, it is that every creature expresses intelligence. Every creature has his or her own story to tell. All we have to do is ask them.

Lessons for Our Lives

Chike and Chuma Chew Walls

CONSIDERING THAT THE TWO YOUNG DOGS WERE BIG FOR their age already, Kirsten and I wondered if she would have her hands full. Kirsten is an intelligent and loving young woman who got both dogs within a week of each other. She rescued them from less than ideal situations. The dogs were both grateful, but they were frisky, playful and a bit wild.

For example, Chuma's favorite after-dinner treat was cell phones. He would grab them off the counter and chew right through them. Chike (pronounced Cheek-ah), on the other hand, preferred bicycle helmets, relishing the snap, crackle and pop of the plastic as she tore them apart piece by piece. In addition, Chike was insistent on chasing the cats, especially Felaki, who until the dogs' arrival had been the "top" animal friend in the household. This was causing Kirsten, the mother of two well-behaved children, to begin to have misgivings about her two ill-behaved canines.

That's when I was called. Kirsten asked if I could talk to them and "lay down the rules"; that is, explain to the dogs that their food, bones, canine toys and the occasional sock were all they were allowed to chew—and that pussy-cats were not for chasing. I always listened to what the dogs had to say and then spoke very firmly to them about the "rules."

First, I tried reason and logic with Chike, explaining why it was not acceptable to chase the cats. "The cats were here first," I reminded her, and added that her behavior was upsetting Kirsten, the kind woman who had given her this lovely new home. But Chike would say things like, "I can't help it," or "It's so much fun!" or " I like to see their fur fly."

The last comment gave me an idea. What if their fur didn't "fly"? I tried a new approach. I talked to the cats instead, especially Felaki. I reminded him that he was the senior, male cat, and suggested that he could try and stand his ground. He should stand up to Chike. And that's exact-ly what he and the other cats did. Instead of turning and running, Felaki, for example, stood still, hissed at Chike and even batted at her with his paws. The chasing stopped.

We were having less success with Kirsten's rules about chewing. I explained the rules to the dogs, but the chewing of "off limits" articles continued. I knew I had to find the root cause of the problem. Quite a bit of money was being spent just trying to keep the house intact. In fact, the dogs had taken to chewing furniture and—believe this—walls!

It was around this time that it occurred to me: these dogs had everything. A beautiful house, toys, bones, loving children to play with and nutritious food to eat. Kirsten even cooked special meals for them. But they just might feel as if they didn't have a purpose. Maybe, I thought, Chike and Chuma needed jobs!

With that in mind, I asked Kirsten what she thought the dogs did best. We agreed that Chike loved being inside the house, and that her "job" would be to guard the inside of the house and the children. Chuma, on the other hand, loved to romp in the yard during the day, so his "job," when he was outside, would be to guard the outside of the house and its environs.

I suggested to Kirsten that she should compliment the dogs each night after they did a good day's work. In the meantime, I kept sending Chike and Chuma thoughts and mental pictures about keeping the house intact. We made sure we all took our assignments very seriously.

Within about a week, the dogs stopped chewing the furniture and the walls. For good. Occasionally now they get a shoe, or a sandal, but no helmets, cell phones or furniture. The key is that they needed a purpose.

And don't we all? Isn't our sense of worth tied to a purpose? We each have a unique purpose here on this earth. Many of us are trying to figure out what that is! Those of us who believe that our purpose is making even one person a day smile, or helping one animal have a better life, well, we are the happy ones. Maybe we don't have the frustration that some people exhibit by punching holes in walls, or Chike and Chuma manifested by chewing on them.

Kirsten, in her wisdom, gave Chike and Chuma jobs they could excel at. And this, more than all her care and attention, convinced them that they have a purpose. They know now that they have value. In short, they are two very satisfied doggies!

Stanley Stays!

THE ABC WORLD NEWS CAMERA CREW WAS ABOUT TO arrive any minute for a field shoot when the phone rang. The call was from Sarah, a client who lives in a multiple-animal household. She wanted to know if I would make an immediate house visit. Her "main man" hadn't eaten for a week and was listless, she said. I asked the TV crew if they would reroute their travel schedule. They didn't mind at all, so off we went to talk to Stanley the turtle.

When we arrived, I put my face level with Stanley, and mentally prepared myself for a serious conversation with the tiny terrapin. However, Stanley apparently found the sight of me anything but serious. He looked me right in the eyes and declared: "You have a big head!" I felt a bit embarrassed to relate this to Sarah, with the crew filming and all, but it's my policy to relate everything the animal friend says, so I did. The camera crew almost rolled on the ground. And no doubt, Stanley was right. From his perspective, my head was huge!

But things became more serious when he told me why he felt the way he did. Then I understood. In Stanley's twenty-seventh year, his guardian, John, had given him to Sarah. He had done it for Stanley's own good, or so he thought—he was getting remarried, and his new partner would be bringing two large dogs into the household. John thought all these new stresses would be difficult for Stanley, and that Sarah had a better household for him and could devote more time to him.

That was all well and good, but Stanley missed his former guardian. Think about it. After twenty-seven years of living with someone, most of us would get used to that person, too, and feel bereaved if we were separated. Not only that, but Stanley had gone from being, by and large, an "only child" to living in a household where interaction among species was common and encouraged.

For example, Sarah thought it would be visually inspiring for Stanley to live right next to her fish. But Stanley appeared apprehensive. He sent me a picture of Sarah's many swimming friends. Apparently, all that undulating made him nervous. For extra company, Sarah had given Stanley the privilege of having his tank in the same room with the parakeets, but their chatter seemed to bother him. Another thing that made Stanley anxious was Chloe, Sarah's dog, who naturally barked from time to time. "Too much," Stanley lamented.

"Is there anything else you want to tell me?" I asked. He practically wailed his reply: the floor in Sarah's apartment was driving him crazy. "It shakes all the time!" he complained. Sarah lives on a busy street with lots of car and truck vibrations that cause the widows and floor to resonate. The combined trauma of his being given away, suddenly having to interact with other species and feeling the floor tremors made him sad, nervous and confused. No wonder he wasn't eating.

So Sarah sprang into action. She piled rugs and towels underneath his tank and placed it in a sunny room a little farther away from the fish, the birds and the vibrating window. From his new spot, it was safe for Stanley to come out and crawl around when and where he liked. I explained the situation to Chloe (a very empathetic creature) who understood about Stanley's aversion to vibrations and noticeably cut back on her barking.

Finally, when the opportunity came, Sarah took Stanley on a two-hour drive to see John. Stanley remained with him for a while and observed all the changes that had occurred in his former home. Ultimately, he asked to come back to stay with Sarah, who drove right over again to bring him back.

Stanley is eating now. He crawls up and down the hallways with Chloe and looks like the big white pit bull's little brown shadow. He's even getting used to the birds chirping. He triumphed over adaptation, sadness, nervousness and confusion.

Stanley is like a lot of us. He got used to what *was*, and had a hard time adjusting to what *is*. Only when he got an opportunity to "go back" did he realize what a good deal he had—and has—living with Sarah. Unlike Stanley, most of us will never have the opportunity to return to a former lifestyle, a former home, a former job. It makes me wonder—how many of us can find the good in what we have here and now?

Honey and the Hurtful Hearsay

ANIMALS COMMUNICATE WITH EACH OTHER ALL THE time—not only within the same species, but from species to species. It's no wonder then, that they are amenable to communicating with us—after all, we're just another species! And animals do love to communicate. In multiple-animal households, I often get calls about one cat attacking another, or one dog picking on another dog. The dog or cat who is seen as the aggressor is the one who often gets the scolding from the human, but I have learned that it's better for me to ask and find out the whole story first, before I talk firmly to any one individual creature. Many, many times, I have learned that the animal who seems so innocent goads and teases the apparent aggressor into a fight.

Sometimes I feel like an old-fashioned principal breaking up a schoolyard fight. I have to get to the bottom of a story, try to ferret out old grudges and encourage both sides to shake paws and make up. Sometimes I need to point out to the human that it is his or her responsibility to try to love each animal equally, and to try to help defend an animal who is being bullied. When the human finally sticks up for the "underdog," the bullying animal often backs off, and for the first time in years, the bullied animal has some peace.

It didn't take me long to figure out that some such intervention might be needed in Honey's case.

Honey is a horse true to her name, a beautiful golden Palomino with a disposition sweet enough to cheer the bitterest heart. That's why her guardian, Mary, was truly surprised when Honey started to act as rambunctious as a teenage rebel. "Something really weird is happening with Honey," Mary told me, worried. "She gets upset during our training sessions and is becoming hard to handle." These behaviors, puzzling in Mary's beloved horse, also could have been dangerous to Mary, because a rider's life can depend on how well the horse responds to his or her subtle commands.

I had spoken to Honey before, and I knew she was a demure horse, a real lady. So when I spoke with her this time, I knew to pay attention to even the most seemingly inconsequential detail of her communication. When she began to talk about the other horses in her stable, I realized that she had recently been moved to a new location. These other horses, she commented, were very big. They were huge bay and chestnut-colored horses, and many of them were thoroughbreds. "They do not look like me at all," Honey said.

Then Honey started to tell me that the other horses made fun of her and her beautiful coat. They said she was very ugly. The ringleader, she said, was a horse whose name, it sounded like to me, began with the letter "P." This horse was Honey's chief tormenter. She and the other horses made fun of Honey for her winning character, calling her insulting and demeaning names because she never gave Mary any flak. Day in and day out she was being assailed. There was no way to get away from those big bullies, since they were in all the stalls next to her. So Honey became influenced.

Mary was understandably upset when I explained what was happening: Honey was going along with the gang. She had to. Her life would be miserable if she didn't. And yes,

Mary confirmed, there was a horse in the stable whose name began with the letter "P."

I explained to Honey that the other horses were jealous of her beauty and her agreeable nature. I asked her if she realized what was happening. The other horses had so cleverly fooled her into believing she was ugly that her self-esteem had plummeted. That's when the other horses' teasing had taken root in her consciousness.

Very shortly after our conversation, Mary moved Honey to a different stable. Honey was immediately much happier, and her sweetness returned. Mary said the turnaround in attitude was rapid and dramatic.

It seems the old adage of being careful of the company one keeps applies not only to humans. Whom do we invite to be our companions? People who support us, or people who can't even support and respect themselves? And what kind of thoughts do we allow to keep us company? Happy, healthy, supporting thoughts? Or thoughts that gang up on us and pull us down until our self-esteem is so low that we become someone else, trying to please others and giving up our own true self in the process?

Courageous Catelda

THE WEEK BEFORE CHRISTMAS, 2000, TEMPERATURES WERE below zero with the wind chill, and Catelda the cat was lost. I had spoken with Catelda before, but her home life was different now, she said. In fact, she was so unhappy with her domestic situation, she had actually run away. And she wasn't coming back until she got some things she really needed in order for her life to be happier. Imagine. A feline negotiator!

Catelda's favorite human companion, Harriet, a young woman in her twenties, had recently moved out of the house. It was just too difficult for her to stay with her parents, who were going through an awkward time. Unfortunately, Harriet couldn't take Catelda to her new apartment. But it seems Catelda, too, was having a stressful time with the emotions that were going on in the household. Catelda wanted her own place to stay, a quiet area where she wouldn't be disturbed and could get away from the commotion when she needed to. She needed "space"— just like Harriet. So Catelda took the situation into her own paws and decided to move to the only place within reach that met her requirements. And, while she was in her place of seclusion, Catelda asked for what I call a "wish list" before she would return home. Once she was satisfied that all her conditions would be met—a bit of peace and quiet, and regular visits from Harriet—she began to send me messages so that I could help her family discover her location.

Working with Catelda required a somewhat different technique than I usually utilize. Catelda wasn't "talking" much about her location, but she sent me mental pictures of where she was and what she saw. It looked to me as though the pictures were coming from a storage room or basement. When I asked Harriet if there was a basement in her parents' house, she replied that there was, and that she and her brother had looked very carefully for Catelda down there. No Catelda.

But Catelda continued to send me pictures of rocks and pipes, and something else: terrible smells! Then I was intuitively guided to ask if there was a *sub*-basement. Bingo. The sub-basement, it turned out, was actually a crawl space that apparently had been used by the family's cats for some time. For lots of different things. Because the odor was so unpleasant, Harriet looked as quickly as possible and, with the aid of a flashlight, confirmed that Catelda must have been sending me images of that very space. The runaway cat, however, was still nowhere to be found.

On day three, a few days before Christmas, the temperatures hit a new low, as did my spirits. Lost animal cases are difficult ones for me, because the human companions and the animals themselves are often quite emotional about not being with each other. In this case, the urgency to find Catelda quickly was foremost in my consciousness, and after three days, I was concerned. I went to a Christmas concert to cheer myself up. Imagine my surprise when, in this pristine, exquisite chapel, I started smelling gasoline! I discreetly asked my husband whether he noticed the odor, but, although his nose can usually detect even the faintest aroma, he didn't smell anything unusual. Eventually, I realized that Catelda was making me aware of something unusual she was smelling in her hiding place.

I called Harriet and asked her to check the crawl space again. Armed with cell phones and flashlights, she and her brother hurried down. Sure enough, there was a distinct smell of gasoline. But with the weather so cold, it was hard for me to imagine how Catelda could be alive . . . except . . . insulation! Again, I was guided to "see" through Catelda's eyes. She showed me a blue box and a red pipe. As I described Catelda's surroundings into the telephone, Harriet and her brother pinpointed Catelda's exact location in the sub-basement wall's insulation. Harriet thought she might have heard a soft mewing. And then all of a sudden it was over. No more communication from Catelda.

About ten minutes later I got a call from Harriet. Apparently there had been a way for Catelda to escape through the insulation to the safety of a bush just outside the house. When Harriet followed the mewing, she found Catelda under the bush—and she was warm.

When I first began my communication with Catelda, I figured she had some pretty strong reasons for staying away if the freezing temperatures weren't bringing her home. So

I asked her what it would take to make her surface and return. And before she would agree to come back, I had to get a commitment from Harriet to do the things Catelda had asked for. This was a little harder than it might seem at first, because Harriet in turn had to convince her family to commit to Catelda's requests, so that her animal friend would have the peace and comfort she sought over the long term. Once everyone had agreed, and I told Catelda, then she allowed us to find her through her "eyes."

One of the saddest things I see in my work is when a human promises an animal friend something that the animal asks for, and then, when the animal friend keeps his or her end of the bargain, for one reason or another the human fails to come through. The animal friend, who had high hopes and bargained in good faith and trust, is sadly disappointed and loses some of that all-important trust. That is why I make a point during human and animal friend negotiations to ask people several times—before I convey their promise to the animal friend—if they are really going to keep that promise. I ask them to carefully consider whether their lifestyle and time schedule will permit them to do what the animal asks of them. Fortunately, Catelda's story ended happily. Harriet, upon Catelda's request, has regular visits now to her parents' house so that she can see Catelda. Catelda has a space she feels more secure about, and the situation at home has calmed quite a bit.

Catelda knew what she wanted in order to make her life bearable. Interestingly, these were the same things Harriet wanted. It still amazes me how much of our emotions our animal friends pick up on. But why should we be amazed? Animals are intelligent, feeling creatures who deserve our respect. And, as Catelda proved, they can exhibit tremendous courage. Catelda braved inconvenience and unpleasant circumstances until she was satisfied that her meager wish list would be met. I wonder how many of us would display that kind of courage to get what we need?

Belle Barks in the Bedroom

BELLE BARKED AT EVERYTHING, IT SEEMED. SHE BARKED AT animals in the yard, she barked at street cleaners, she barked at lightning. Especially, Barbara said, Belle barked in the bedroom. In fact, at eight o'clock p.m. on any given night, Belle would go up to the bedroom, *stare at a particular wall* and bark. Nothing seemed to help—Belle would bark until she wore herself out, and the noise was very upsetting to Barbara.

This was interesting! First I asked Belle about the barking during thunderstorms, which Barbara said was pre-

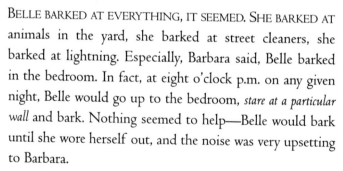

dictable, loud and continuous. Belle answered by telling me something about her history. Belle had been purchased from a pet store, where she had never, ever been able to sleep. Just when she settled in and started to relax, BOOM! A dog would start barking, and then the whole lot of dogs would start. Now, even though Belle was Barbara's only dog, the startling noise from the thunder still gave her a jolt, especially when she was sleeping. Then she would remember her pet store days and just keep barking. She took the thunder as a personal assault on her, as if something or someone was conspiring to disturb her sleep.

I empathized with her. Being in the profession that I'm in, I find I do quite a bit of work at night. This is often when animals feel most comfortable communicating. Between the hours of two and five a.m., community thought is generally quiet, and I can receive the animals' thoughts with less interference. And they know it. So I frequently wake at two a.m. and know intuitively that it's time for me to get to work. It's not often that I sleep through the night. So I knew how Belle felt.

I told her this, and then explained that the thunder would not hurt her. She was safe inside a beautiful house with a caring companion. Although the sound was startling, she could relax in knowing that no physical harm would come her way because of the storm.

And what about barking at the wall every night at eight p.m.? That turned out to be easy. Barbara had a flickering light on the wall, and Belle barked at the movement, trying to warn Barbara that something was there that could potentially harm them both. Once again, I explained to Belle that she was safe, and that Barbara knew about the flickering motion of the light. However, I also suggested to Barbara that she change the light to something less threatening for Belle.

As far as the animals in the yard, Belle gave a surprising answer. She barked at the birds and the squirrels because she was mad at them! When Barbara first brought Belle home with her, the little terrier enjoyed her new yard. She ran up to the birds and squirrels, not wanting to hurt them, but wanting to play with them and make friends. Her intentions were innocent and pure, but the other animals ran away in fear. Then, just like a person who has been rebuffed, Belle began to resent their not wanting to be friends with her. Now she barked at them to warn them away from the yard: if they wouldn't play with her, they weren't welcome.

I explained to Belle she was so much bigger than these other creatures that it was "normal" for them to fly and run away. They probably did not understand that she wanted to be their friend. I suggested that she should not take their rebuff personally and asked if she could see things from their perspective.

Finally, Belle revealed to me that she was a bit insecure. Even though on the outside she portrayed the brave, sturdy Scottish terrier, inside was a doggie who was always waiting "for the other shoe to drop," so to speak. And it wasn't because she was treated poorly. It was because she was treated so well. As a matter of fact, Belle had a hard time believing her good fortune in having a home with Barbara! In turn, Barbara wondered if Belle really loved her and had a good time with her. It was easy to see that Belle held back a little part of her love, always thinking that perhaps Barbara would get rid of her because of that unceasing barking. Belle told me she knew the barking bothered Barbara, but until now she felt she couldn't help it. Belle was ashamed of herself and feared that her behavior was jeopardizing her relationship with Barbara.

I agreed that the barking did, indeed, annoy Barbara, but most importantly, I stressed something that a doggie could truly understand: her loud barking hurt Barbara's ears. Belle really took note of this! Meanwhile, having seen that Belle yearned for more activity and companionship with other animal friends, I suggested a doggie camp to Barbara, where there would be lots of different activities for Belle to try.

After about three weeks, I got a call from Barbara. Belle's barking had measurably decreased. She hardly barked during thunderstorms now, and when she did, Barbara treated her to hugs, pats and an occasional doggie treat. That certainly calmed her. Most all of, however, I think Barbara was calmer, now that she understood what her little doggie had gone through.

Once Barbara found out more about Belle's insecurities, she did the absolute smartest thing: she worked on her own! Barbara admitted that she, too, always worried about "the other shoe dropping"—that if she got too close to another person, her feelings might be hurt. She noticed that after she had worked very hard on this personal issue for only two weeks, the change in Belle was astounding!

All in all, Belle is a happier doggie, Barbara sleeps better at night, and these two wonderful creatures have a closer connection than before. Belle has just received a diploma from the doggie camp she went to, and has expressed satisfaction about making her "mom" proud by doing a little agility training and just having a good time—a combination that will surely increase her sense of self worth. For her part, Barbara was so impressed with the change her own self-exploration produced in Belle that she suggested I write a book about how people's attitudes and beliefs affect their animals' behaviors! She and Belle are living proof that for our animal friends, a little work on ourselves can make all the difference in the world.

Surprising Sessions

Lovely Loren

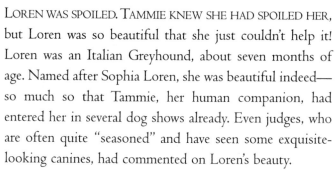

LOREN WAS SPOILED. TAMMIE KNEW SHE HAD SPOILED HER, but Loren was so beautiful that she just couldn't help it! Loren was an Italian Greyhound, about seven months of age. Named after Sophia Loren, she was beautiful indeed— so much so that Tammie, her human companion, had entered her in several dog shows already. Even judges, who are often quite "seasoned" and have seen some exquisite-looking canines, had commented on Loren's beauty.

It seems that her lovely appearance was undisputed. On the show table, in front of judges, however, she was a terror. She was never awarded any prizes, and in one show she misbehaved so much that she was asked to leave!

Tammie was mystified by Loren's behavior and asked me to talk with her. I quickly observed that this lovely little animal was quite perturbed about competing in dog shows. She knew she was beautiful, but the hustle and bustle of the shows made her nervous. She didn't like being around the noisy crowds of people, and she commented on "too many people [i.e., judges] touching me." And she definitely did not want to listen to me try to change her mind!

Loren was convinced that she knew what she wanted: to have a mate and lounge around the house. Not only that, but she already had her eye on a male she fancied: Bruno, a very handsome, congenial Italian Greyhound who Tammie told me was on his way to becoming a blue ribbon champion. Loren was adamant about her choice: no one but Bruno would do.

I explained to Loren that Tammie thought she was so beautiful she wanted the whole world to see her. If she would win just one ribbon, I told her, Tammie had said she could be a stay-at-home doggie. But nothing would convince Loren that her participation in shows was a good idea. As a matter of fact, she became very snippy! I ended the conversation suddenly, saying that when she would talk respectfully to me, as I had to her, we could resume talking. This was the first time I had to stop a conversation because an animal was rude!

I then spoke with Bruno to let him know of Loren's intentions, and what he said startled me. He knew that Loren was very pretty, but he'd be happier, he told me, with someone who was a little nicer, if not so pretty. I repeated this to Loren and it really shook her up! Despite this rebuff, however, she remained determined to have things immediately her way. She never did develop that "Doris Day" disposition—sunny, cheerful, pleasant—and Bruno never did take a shine to her.

But Tammie loved Loren no matter what—and she realized that that meant she had to respect Loren's wishes. There are dogs who enjoy being shown in dog shows and dogs who don't. The dogs who like shows do so for a variety of reasons: some like the challenge, some like to "strut their stuff" so to speak, but the reason I most often hear from the dogs themselves is that it gives them an extended opportunity to be with their guardian or their handler. They cherish the closeness and the bond. But for some, the bright lights, the loud sounds and the abundance of smells are too much. For others, the travel routine involved in being on a show circuit is difficult, since their diet, exercise routines and sleep patterns may change from the ones they have at home. Finally, dogs who have done obedience and conformation shows for years and years often long for something else. Their guardians and handlers often sense the dogs may need a change and ask me to find out the dog's viewpoint. When I talk to one of these dogs, I like to ask the guardian if I can offer some alternatives to his or her canine friend. Most guardians are extremely open to this idea, since they want the best life for their dogs. So I will send the dog a mental picture of himself or herself as an agility dog. Oh! Many dogs love this alternative! They see it as great fun! Or I picture the dog as a therapy dog. Oh! Many dogs perk up at this.

Although remuneration for a consultation comes from the human companion, I feel it is my responsibility, as best I can, to equitably and amicably represent the thoughts and wishes of both the human and non-human to each other. I see it as a sign of respect to both species. In my opinion, that is what this work is all about—helping both the human and animal friend to see things from a slightly different perspective and gain a better understanding of where each is coming from. For Tammie and Loren, this meant that if Loren didn't want to be shown, then Tammie wouldn't show her. Not all of her beautiful dogs, Tammie realized, could be shown when she wanted them to be shown. They had personalities and ideas of their own. Loren adores Tammie, provides great companionship to her and loves being a stay-at-home doggie. And Tammie, as with the vast majority of guardians who utilize my services, just wants her friend, lovely Loren, to be happy.

Puff Puff is Perturbed

Humans seem willing to believe that whales and porpoises can communicate with us, but most people are surprised when I explain that our "at home" fish friends can also communicate. In fact, I have learned that fish are excellent at getting their points across. Take Puff Puff, for example. Puff Puff is not a blowfish as her name might indicate, but a shovelnose catfish—what some might call an "ordinary" fish. She's anything but ordinary, though.

Her guardian, Shelly, asked me to do a consultation with her because "the fish is driving me nuts. She eats all the other fish in the tank. I paid a lot of money for these fish, and, presto, when I come home, they're gone! And she does something else that is *really* driving us crazy. She keeps banging her head against the glass. When my husband and I sit down in the evening and we want to relax, that's all we hear. I'm thinking about having to get rid of her."

When I communicated with Puff Puff, she told me she really liked the tank. And she was quite fond of her "parents," Shelly and Joe—but complained that she hardly ever saw them. And when she did, she lamented, they were playing with their cats! "It's true," Shelly replied. "We've been working really long hours trying to start a new business, and when we come home, we're exhausted. We sit on the couch and try to play with Booka, Cosmic and Cuervo."

Meanwhile, Puff Puff would hit her head repeatedly against the tank, trying to get their attention. In a human, this behavior would be frightening and dangerous. But before we could ask her, Puff Puff volunteered, "No. It doesn't hurt." When I conveyed this to Shelly, she practically jumped out of her chair. "Oh my goodness!" she said. "Joe and I sit and ask each other all the time: 'Doesn't that hurt her head?'" Puff Puff had intuited her human friends' concern.

Then Shelly requested that I ask Puff Puff why she ate the other fish in the tank. "I'm hungry!" she replied. I suggested she feed Puff Puff more. Puff Puff also asked for some visual stimulation—specifically, an image she sent me that looked like a wavy banner with the colors of the rainbow in it. She asked if Shelly could "hang it up in front of the tank." I suppose it reminded Puff Puff of another fish, but she didn't tell me why she wanted it. Shelly found a beautiful, shiny banner that had all the colors Puff Puff had pictured to me. It shimmered whenever the air currents in the house breezed by it, and Puff Puff told me later that she loved it!

After several weeks I spoke with Shelly. She told me that our session had made her look at Puff Puff in an entirely new way. She had never known fish could have feelings like that—could wish for visually inspiring surroundings and attentive friends, and miss them when they went away. And then she told me something that made me smile. When they came home from work that night, Shelly and Joe walked up to Puff Puff's tank. Puff Puff came right to the front and nuzzled the spot right where their fingers were! She did it again and again.

Shelly and Joe have since gotten Puff Puff a friend (whom Puff Puff hasn't eaten, since she now gets all the food she needs), and the whole family of fish, people and felines are getting along very well.

I've connected with plenty of porpoises and dolphins, and they too are wonderful communicators, but it's important to remember that mammals don't have a monopoly on thoughts and feelings! On the contrary, what these consultations have shown me is that we have little marine treasures sitting here right in our living rooms just waiting to be our friends.

The Question of Queen Liliokalani

TAMARA WAS WORRIED ABOUT BEES, IN GENERAL. "THEY are dying," she told me in a plaintive voice. Concerned about the dangerous mites that can infest hives and feed on the bees' larvae, Tamara in her true kindness wanted to raise some honey bees in Illinois—just to help the general population of bees.

Tamara's trouble started when the bee company messed up the order. They sent the bees too early in the spring, before the weather was warm enough for the bees to live

Like the bee pictured here, Queen Liliokalani loved flowers and bright colors.

37

outside. They also sent the bees before they sent the hive! So Tamara had to keep a cardboard box full of swarming bees in her house for about a week, feeding them sugar water and trying not to let too many bees out of the box!

When the hive finally came, Tamara was in for a surprise. It was an "assembly required" wooden hive with about one hundred different parts. So Tamara asked her son and his friends to quickly assemble the hive. Now the only thing that she and her bees needed was for the weather to cooperate. It didn't. April and May in and around Chicago can be very unpredictable; this year the weather was unusually cold. Tamara asked me to reassure the bees that spring was on its way and flowers would be coming out. All would be well. Meanwhile, the cold and rain continued.

I chose to talk with the queen bee. She let me know the journey had been rough and the bees were very cold. They were also upset because they didn't have any flowers to fly to, to gather the nectar and pollen they needed to make honey. Tamara and I bought flower pots filled with beautiful, hardy flowers. We put them right by the bees so they could start making their own honey instead of having Tamara feed them with sugar water.

Despite our best efforts, after a while the queen bee became very quiet, and I was concerned that she might not have recovered from the journey to Illinois and the unseasonable cold. As it turned out, she did not make it.

Tamara knew she needed another queen bee. But she wasn't sure how to introduce a new queen into the hive so that the other bees would accept her. So she went to beekeeper meetings. She researched in libraries and on the Web. She read books. She talked to university scholars. Everyone had their own answers, but we soon had another queen bee on the way. That's when I had the sheer pleasure of meeting Queen Liliokalani.

At first, Tamara kept the queen in the cardboard box the bee company had shipped her in, and I spoke with the other bees about introducing her into the hive. While they waited, Tamara and her newest bee friend picked out a name they both loved: Liliokalani. Queen Liliokalani relished the sound of her name, a name from a warm and flower-filled place—Hawaii. Once I tried to call her Queen Lil when I spoke to her, but she would have none of that! The queen also loved music, so Tamara sang to her whenever she could.

Queen Liliokalani seemed sensitive to color as well as sound. She was very feminine and asked for flowers and bright colors. Perhaps she had had a colorful environment on the bee-raising farm. She told me she hated the large purple spot that the bee company had marked on her in order to tell her apart from the other bees. I said perhaps it was a food dye and would wear off. Queen Liliokalani liked that.

The queen looked forward to having warm weather and kind bees to be with. She also asked an unusual question: "Will I ever be allowed out of the hive once I go in?" At first, I didn't know what to tell Queen Liliokalani. I had always thought that once queens went in, they never came out. I had to consult with the hive and ask them many questions. Would they accept her? Would they let her out every so often? Would they be nice to her?

I discovered that there was a small but strong group that really didn't want a new queen. I tried reasoning with them, bargaining, telling them it was for the good of the hive—but they were recalcitrant. The vast majority of the bees, however, sincerely wanted her, and the "opposition" finally told me that they would try to live in harmony with the new queen. I got the feeling that they were waiting to see if she measured up.

The message came not a moment too soon, because Queen Liliokalani appeared to be claustrophobic. She couldn't stand being in the small cardboard box, and felt she couldn't take it any longer. Tamara had no choice but to introduce her into the hive immediately.

No sooner had we done that than the small opposing group started to attack Queen Liliokalani. By the time the other bees managed to fend them off, the queen seemed very weak. I scolded and cajoled the attackers. Once again I bargained with them. Once again they said they would try to live in harmony.

Queen Liliokalani tried to relax, but she soon let me know that things were stirring up again in the hive. The "opposition" really never accepted her, and she believed they were planning to attack her again. If that happened, she told me, she didn't think she'd survive. One day she told me that she and some of the other bees were planning to leave the hive.

My friend Tamara was busy working three jobs and caring for her household, her other animal friends and now her bees. She continued to sing lovingly to Queen Liliokalani, but about a week after my last communication with the queen, Tamara called to tell me the bees had gone, all but a small group.

I learned a lot of lessons from this case. First, the queen demanded respect. She would not let me call her Queen Lil. She let me know right away that she didn't like that. How many humans let their bosses or co-workers or family members say things to them they really don't want to hear? Many people let themselves be called names they would prefer others not use, but they never stick up for themselves. The queen did.

I also learned from the queen that we shouldn't stay where we're not wanted. I believe this is a lesson that many humans can learn as well. How many people stay in abusive situations where they feel there is some animosity toward them? Perhaps there are times and situations where it is more than a feeling. Some people stay in situations after they have been physically or mentally attacked. I believe we should be like the queen and try to stick it out, giving the situation the best that we can (she seemed to do her "job" of being a queen, and was always busy whenever I talked to her) but after a while, when it still doesn't feel right or we feel we're about to lose our health over an inharmonious work (or family-oriented) situation, we should consider disrupting the norm (in this case the hive) and flying away. As fast as we can. That's what the queen did.

Finally, people ask me all the time if a horse is "smarter" than a dog, if a dog is smarter than a cat, if a cat is smarter than a bird, if a bird is smarter than a frog, etc. They always list the animals in the same order, starting with what they assume is a larger-brained and more intelligent animal. I've learned, and my conversations with the queen confirmed, that communication from non-humans has nothing to do with the size of an animal's brain. It has to do with mutual respect from one species to another. In my consultations, I communicate with a bee or a moth or an ant the same way I communicate with a horse or a dog, a human or a lizard. I try to do it with respect and the understanding that they are sentient, intelligent creatures. And this is why I think I intuitively hear or feel or see a lot from insects. I *expect* to hear or feel or see a lot.

I never heard from Queen Liliokalani again. It was still warm enough for her to find a new place and establish a new hive, but there appears to be so much energy that gets put into creating a new hive that I don't know if the bees could have managed it. I hope the queen found a place to "over" winter, but I will never forget how feminine she was, how she wanted beauty all around her, and how Soul-filled that small divine creature was.

Bewildering Behaviors

Nicky Never Knew

THREE DAYS BEFORE CHRISTMAS, NICKY WAS JETTED across the United States from a breeder to his new home in the Midwest. His family instantly fell in love with him, and soon Nicky became the center of attention and the prince of the house—a big, beautiful house, with cushy seats for the little Lhasa Apso to sit on, and lots of sunshine to light his day.

But there was a problem: despite being lovingly house-trained, ever since Nicky came to the family, he had been wetting occasionally in the house. The condition gradually worsened, until he was regularly wetting his "mom's" favorite Persian rug—right in the middle of the room. It was difficult not to notice.

In my experience as an animal communicator, I have found that there are many reasons why a dog may urinate in the house. The most common include physical maladies, fear that the guardian won't return, what I call "My smell is best" and "intruder smells." "My smell is best" usually means that there are other animals of the same species or different species in the house; the dog or cat in question will often urinate to cover up the other animals' odors so that his or her own smell predominates. And an animal may notice "intruder smells" when the guardian carries other animals' smells in from the outside on his or her clothes.

When I spoke with Nicky's "mom," Grace, she told me that Nicky had everything a doggie could want. She just didn't understand what Nicky was trying to say. It turned out that Nicky had a lot to say.

His family was coming and going, he said. People came and they left. He didn't know what was going on, and this confused him. The family had seemed so stable during his first couple of months with them, and he had thought it would always be that way. But things had changed. The nice big house Nicky lived in required money to maintain. His mom had an important job now, and his brothers and dad were mostly off at college or work. Nicky was no longer the center of attention. He was just a part of a very busy family.

I thought Nicky's wetting might be a sign of mild separation anxiety. On top of this, however, he told me that he had never really understood his housetraining. What did his family want of him? It was still a mystery to him after all this time. No wonder he wet in the house! The case wasn't just one of separation anxiety, it was one of a dog not having understood what was expected of him. He just didn't know. So when he wanted more attention, and sought it the best way he knew how—wetting a favorite rug—he didn't realize that he was also breaking a household rule.

When I told Grace this, she confirmed that only one of her sons still lived at home, and that her family was incredibly busy. Still, she said, Nicky spent a lot of time at night on their laps. I asked her if she and her husband were busy doing other things at this time, too. She agreed that this was so.

Then I suggested a few easy changes. During the day, even as little as fifteen minutes of play with Nicky would make a big difference. After their son came home from school, instead of letting Nicky out to urinate in the back yard (after which he would just come in the house and urinate) he should take Nicky for a walk. When they spent time with Nicky in the evening, they should really focus on him. A shorter amount of "quality time" would provide the dog with a much-needed sense of recognition.

Most importantly, the family members could try to see things from the little dog's standpoint. I likened his experience to going to a big party, where everyone but you seems to be having a wonderful time. Maybe it just takes one person at that party to show some caring, sincere, focused attention, and you'll come away feeling you had a good time. That's what was needed in Nicky's life: some extra caring, some focused attention, and a little playtime. Sounds like a prescription for many of us in today's busy life.

Manny the Manic Macaw

MANNY WAS THE MOST BEAUTIFUL BIRD I HAD EVER SEEN. His guardian, Phyllis, thought so, too. But right from the start she let me know that if the problems she was having with Manny couldn't be solved, she wouldn't be able to keep him. This was an especially upsetting prospect because in two former households, Manny had been severely mistreated, locked in dark closets for days at a time. Phyllis truly loved him and wanted to keep him from ever getting into the wrong hands again.

Then she told me some of the problems she and Manny were having. Since they had moved into a new apartment, the macaw had seemed depressed, nervous and anxious. Before the move, they had lived with Phyllis's family and there had always been someone around to keep Manny company. But since the move, Manny spent hours alone each day while Phyllis was at work—and he had taken to yelling at the top of his little birdie lungs whenever she left the house. Phyllis feared the neighbors would start complaining, and her new apartment was so conveniently close to her job that she hated to think that she might be forced to move. So she wanted to know if Manny would be willing to stop his wailing and screeching.

I've found that asking the animals *why* they are doing some particular behavior is usually the key to changing that behavior. So I simply asked Manny why he was doing what he did. He explained that in addition to the fear of being alone, he couldn't stand the slamming and thudding noises that went on all day and night. They were driving him to distraction. I asked Phyllis about this and she identified the noises right away. She was on the top floor of the building she said and she, too, heard the vents on the roof spring open and thump shut at all hours. Her own hallway was particularly noisy, because three of the families who shared it slammed doors whenever they left their apartments—so loudly that even some of the other humans on the floor had recently complained to the management company.

I explained to Manny what the noises were and let him know that Phyllis and the other tenants were trying to put a stop to the slamming doors. The sounds bothered them too, I said. The noises from the vents on the roof were a harder problem to solve, but Phyllis said that she could move Manny's cage, which now stood directly under one of the vents, and try to dampen the noise by affixing a quilt to the ceiling.

Noise wasn't Manny's only concern. There was also the cat smell. No, Phyllis didn't have a cat. But the representative of the management company may have had one. Manny said that a man had been in the apartment several times, and that the man had smelled of cat! Phyllis admitted that the management company did have a key and had been known to perform routine inspections. Not only that, but the people who had previously lived in the apartment had had cats. No matter what the source, the cat smell was making Manny very anxious. And who could blame him? We have to remember that our animal friends' sense of smell and hearing is often much better than ours. Phyllis may not have noticed a cat smell, but Manny did, and he felt very threatened. When he made noise, he was crying out in fear.

Then Manny admitted that as much as he loved Phyllis,

he missed living with all her nice brothers. who always told him how handsome he was. Now almost no one came over, and he had nothing to do when Phyllis was at work. He just sat in his cage and heard frightening sounds and smelled threatening smells. No wonder he didn't want Phyllis to leave in the mornings!

Clearly Manny needed a distraction. I suggested that Phyllis leave a radio talk show on, or a videotape playing, so that Manny could hear human voices or see movement. If she had the funds, perhaps she could hire someone to bird-sit on certain days—just to come over during a lunch hour and keep Manny company. I also suggested that maybe she could have more friends or family over to visit, so that Manny could be complimented again.

Several weeks later I received a call from Phyllis. Her job was transferring her! Now she was more than willing to leave that apartment, and she asked if I would tell Manny that she would be looking for a new place for them to live. I swear I could feel the pent-up tension drain out of that bird's body.

Was it coincidence that Phyllis was asked to move again for her job? Was it part of a grand plan the Universe had for her to get Manny out of that building? I don't know. What I do know is that Phyllis is now aware of what Manny needs in order to be calmer, and that she will do just about anything to make that beautiful bird happy. Maybe the Universe just gave her a little nudge.

Queenie Gets Quiet

IT WAS THE DAY BEFORE THE MOVERS WERE SCHEDULED TO put all our possessions into a huge van and roll them down the highway to our new home. How, I wondered, could two adults, four cats and one dog amass twelve thousand pounds of "stuff"? Just the thought of unpacking it all made me tired. Then the phone rang. My next-door neighbor was calling to say goodbye . . . and "By the way, could you do me a favor?"

It turned out that the "favor" she wanted was an emergency animal communication consultation for her boss—a lovely lady who was on the verge of euthanizing a cat named Queenie if she couldn't find out why Queenie was acting the way she did!

With the stress of the move and all that was going on, I felt I didn't need another pressured or "emergency" case right then. But I thought of the possible outcomes if I didn't take the case, and I agreed I would call Diana, Queenie's guardian, to see what I could do.

Diana turned out to be a willing client, but she had little idea of what an animal communicator did. I talked to her about the process very openly and thoroughly, and asked her if she wanted some assistance. "Yes!" she replied. Diana explained the problem: Queenie was urinating not in her cat box, but in odd places. Cello cases, upholstered chairs and rugs. Diana liked the pussycat, but the problem had gotten totally out of hand.

Diana seemed to be a lady who observed things very well, and I could see she had really tried to piece together on her own why Queenie urinated all over. She said they had recently moved into their current house and maybe it wasn't what Queenie had been accustomed to, because the urinating had began shortly after they had moved in.

Still, before I could give my own analysis, I needed to speak directly and lovingly to Queenie. I asked if she liked her cat litter. "Is it too hard?" I asked. No, she replied, it was "all right." What about her food? I asked if she was happy with it. "It is all right." Hmm, I thought. Not exactly exuberant answers, but she doesn't seem too dissatisfied, either.

Then I asked her about her family and her house. Queenie told me that she liked the people in the family, but disliked the noises they made! For example, Queenie hated when the children played their instruments—they were "too noisy." She didn't like the children's yelling— "too loud"—and she didn't like the sounds that came out of the TV or the stereo. (She sent me car siren sounds and violin sounds—presumably from these appliances' speakers.) Diana verified that her children were normal teens and preteens, and yes, they did make a fair amount of noise. They certainly practiced their instruments, but despite Queenie's aversion to the sounds they made, Diana didn't want to encourage them to stop! On an intuition, I asked Diana if I could talk with Queenie again. Diana was happy to get additional information that would help the family and the feline.

I remembered Diana's comment about the new house being a change for Queenie. On a hunch, I asked Queenie if she had had another guardian before coming to Diana's. Almost with a sigh, she told me of her life with an elderly lady and many other animals in a house where she had been happy. But one day the lady left the front door open and Queenie just walked out. Just for the heck of it. Just so an indoor cat could see the outdoor world.

Many cats have the same desire, and when they get the chance, they go. Then they realize they've gone too far, and some have problems getting back. Then they, and their guardians, panic. When I talk with them, the vast majority of animal friends want to return home, and they do. But others are too hot, or too confused, or too tired, and that is what had happened to Queenie. She just got confused and lost, and like many runaway indoor cats, she wasn't wearing a collar. Someone brought her to an animal shelter, and Diana and her family got her from there.

When I shared Queenie's history with Diana, she remembered that her veterinarian had an elderly friend who lived on a farm and was looking for a barn cat! It sounded like a good environment for Queenie—she could have animal friends and an elderly human companion again, and the barn would be free of stereos and musical instruments! And indeed, Queenie was very happy after her move. Although she heard loud sounds sometimes (the sounds she sent me were loud rumbling sounds), she could get away from the sounds when she wanted to. This made her very happy, indeed.

In Queenie's case, when a new home was needed, it was immediately available. This is not always the case. Placing an animal in a new home often requires effort and patience. Yet it must be done. When we adopt an animal friend, we assume responsibility for his or her physical, mental and emotional welfare. If we can no longer care for that friend, we must call upon our integrity, honor and kindness in finding them a new, suitable home. After all, as seen throughout these stories, these are the qualities they display toward us.

In over ninety-five percent of the cases I handle, both the animal and the human come to understand what is expected of them. When the human can see the animal as a partner, then the going is easier, the results are better, and the relationship can be renewed and refreshed. This partnership helps both the human and the animal learn the lessons they need to learn. But there are times when, no matter what the human does, the relationship just doesn't seem to work. Then it is time to part ways. The decision can be an agonizing one. The same types of questions emerge from many peoples' consciousness: Did I do enough? Could I have tried one more thing?

When I get these types of questions all I can say is this: You'll know. It's the same as a relationship with another human. Like a passenger on a sinking ship, you stay with it until you know that it will pull you down, too. Then you know you can't sacrifice your life or your happiness any more to keep it afloat. You let it go with a loving heart and blessings. Letting go is never easy. But perhaps it is the only sane way. In the end, if it truly blesses you spiritually, it will bless your animal companion spiritually. Just like Queenie when she parted ways from Diana's family and entered a new life where she could get what she had wanted all along: quiet.

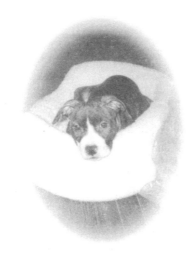

Duke Defends Damsels

SANDRA, AN EXPERT DOG TRAINER, HAD ANTICIPATED that her new dog, Duke, would become the shining example of good behavior in her dog training classes. Instead, Duke got into fights with just about every dog that came too close to Sandra. Exasperated, Sandra called me. She explained that she had gotten Duke from a very good friend of hers, a dog breeder named Sergio. Sergio and his wife, Patricia, had given Duke to Sandra out of empathy not long after her beloved dog Howie had passed. Duke was Sergio's favorite out of all the litter, and Sergio considered that he and Duke had become good friends. That was why Duke was such a valuable gift from Sergio to Sandra.

When I spoke with Duke, an American Staffordshire terrier, he said that he was confused and very sad. He was extremely fond of Sergio, the breeder, but mostly he adored Patricia. The three of them had been very amiable companions, and Duke wondered why they had given him away. Duke was also sad because he couldn't figure out where all his brothers and sisters had gone. He had grown extremely close to his littermates, and couldn't understand why they didn't frolic and play together anymore.

Then he said something that really made my ears perk up: that he had been hit or hurt on his left side by a man, about twenty to thirty years old, when he was living with the breeder. He even "showed" me the colors of the furniture that were in the room where it happened. Duke also told me that his mother had been hurt on her side when he was very little. He remembered being frightened about this. Something else frightened him, too. He stated that his friend Sergio, whom he loved very much, sometimes spoke very firmly to Patricia, and that this alarmed him.

By now, I was feeling rather alarmed myself, but I needed verification from Sandra before I felt comfortable proceeding. While I didn't want to say anything detrimental about her good friend, the breeder, my obligation as an animal communicator compelled me to tell her the whole of what Duke had said.

Sandra wasn't sure what to do. Should she approach her friend directly, she wondered, or try to bring these points up subtly during future conversations? She decided to be discreet but direct, and managed to shed some light on Duke's statements after speaking with Sergio.

Patricia, a veterinarian, confirmed that Duke's mom had been very active up to the day she had her litter and might have fallen or bumped into furniture in the house. As far as Duke having been hurt on his left side, she said that when they were scrutinizing buyers for the littermates, one fellow, about twenty to thirty years old, had held and dropped Duke. They asked the man to leave their house immediately, figuring that he wasn't a good candidate for purchasing one of their pups. As far as the colors of the furniture in the living room, where this had happened, Duke had been right on target.

I then told Sandra about Duke's unusually strong grief over the sale of his littermates. In truth, I had never heard a dog speak so forlornly about being separated from his littermates. Specifically, Duke had said that every day he saw people come into his home and take his brothers and sisters away. Sometimes other dogs would come and take his littermates away, too! This left him feeling angry and morose. Sergio confirmed that he had arranged for placement of Duke's littermates, and that prospective guardians had indeed come to their house to take Duke's brothers and sisters away. He corroborated that sometimes the prospective guardians brought their dogs with them, in order to see if the dog they wanted would get along with the dog they had. Duke had been the last dog at home, so he really did see all his brothers and sisters disappear.

When Sandra told Sergio about Duke's being frightened sometimes by the firm tone of his voice, Sergio laughed and said, "Duke talks too much!" As a dog breeder, it was important for Sergio to keep all the dogs in line at home; the firm tone he used was to get his wife's attention when the doggies were too unruly. His wife remembered, however, that Duke would make little growling sounds and come to her side when this happened, as if to defend her.

So how did this figure into Duke's aggression with other dogs in Sandra's training class?

It hit me all of a sudden, and I discreetly asked Duke some questions that confirmed the following: Duke was a frightened doggie who felt the need to defend women. When his mother fell, he felt frightened. When Sergio used a firm tone of voice around his wife, Duke was frightened for Patricia and wanted to defend her. In a class situation, Duke growled and attacked because he was protective of Sandra: he wouldn't let her be taken away from him as his own littermates had been taken.

I explained all this to Sandra. She felt relieved but troubled by a new concern—was Duke unhappy in her care? Did he really want to be with her and her housemate? I asked Duke. Yes, he said, Sandra and Harvey treated him very well, and this was his home now. I also explained to him the reason Sergio had given him to Sandra—that he was the best gift Sergio knew to give. Duke was pleased with that.

Sandra tried an experiment about a week after this. She invited Sergio and Patricia to her home. Duke was very glad to see his old friends, but when they left, he did not mourn. And now that Sandra knows more about what Duke went through as a little puppy, she and Harvey have more empathy for him. Being the excellent trainer she is, she recognized that a class situation was too stressful for Duke and decided to train him in real life situations instead. We both agreed that Duke would go to the classes when and if he was ready. Until then, he can be the shining example of good behavior right in Sandra's living room.

I have learned that there is always a reason why our animal friends act the way they do. Many people in this instance would not have reacted the same way Sandra did. Many people, when they feel they have a "biter" on their hands, will hit or scold the animal, or give him or her away.

The two most frequent types of cases I get are dog biting cases and cat litter-box problem cases. In the cases of dog biting, I have learned that in most instances, the issue is not just aggression but mainly fear—that is, the dog's fear for his or her own safety or for the safety of his or her guardian. I have learned that it is therapeutic for the animal to tell me about his or her own feelings and his or her story personally. It's like talking to a friend, someone who won't scold or judge. (And I try to never, ever do either.) After the animal communicates the story, in the way he or she knows how, then the guardian finally understands the reason behind the behavior. Then we can take steps to communicate further to the animal friend why he or she doesn't have to fear anymore, or what the human can do to make the animal friend feel safer. Successful animal communication is a two-way street that requires compassion, dedication and labor from both species. The effort and trust is what makes the process beautiful. That's why it works.

What We Think Matters

"Misty's" Miracle

JEANNIE FIRST CALLED ME BECAUSE SHE WAS SAD AND somewhat perplexed about her new horse, Misty, a thirteen-year-old Morgan mare. The horse was acting aloof, Jeannie said. She was hard to bridle and seemed skittish and uncomfortable on her rides through the beautiful countryside. Jeannie wondered if the horse was unhappy with her.

When I asked Misty about her feelings, she had a lot to tell me. She showed me pictures of herself as a young filly that gave me an idea of her former happy life. Her guardians, a mother and daughter, adored her. They praised her constantly and brought apples and scrumptious foods to her pasture. Misty could do no wrong in their eyes, and the happy relationship had gone on for about ten years. But then, all of a sudden, Misty was whisked off her pleasant pasture and sold. She found herself in a new barn with a new guardian. It's little wonder that Misty was beside herself. She wasn't just "aloof," as Jeannie had suggested. Misty was mourning.

Why, Misty asked me, was she here and not with her dear old friends? I consulted Jeannie, who filled in some clues to the puzzle so that I could be accurate in my explanation to Misty. It appears that Misty's former guardians had become strapped for money and simply couldn't afford to care for her any longer. They had loved Misty so much that they couldn't even bring themselves to say their last "good-byes" to her. It was just too painful.

I explained the situation to Misty, reassuring her that her former guardians had really loved her. I also let her know that Jeannie loved her, and that this was the start of a new life for her. I assured Misty that Jeannie said she would always take good care of her, and I asked if Misty could try to make friends with Jeannie. I suggested that Jeannie bring apples and little pieces of apple pie to Misty, spend some quality time with her, and perhaps even sit in her stall and share a meal with her.

Jeannie seemed to like this idea. So in she went every day, toting apples and apple pie. Misty found this very amusing and was pleasantly surprised to see the extent Jeannie would go to be friends with her.

The next time Jeannie checked in with me, though, she said that things had improved, but Misty still seemed skittish and nervous around her. I talked with Misty, who told me that when Jeannie visited, her head was "in a thousand different places." I asked Jeannie if this was true, and she admitted that it was. She said she would be thinking of many other things she had to do while she was visiting Misty. Misty was smart! She would not be fooled into being friends with another being who wasn't trying equally to be friends with her! She wanted Jeannie's entire attention for the friendship to be formed.

I believe this was Misty's great gift to Jeannie. As a result of Misty's observations, Jeannie began to read books on how to concentrate and live in the present. She started to really focus on the friendship and the horse. When she and Misty were together, she refused to allow her attention to wander. And Misty felt this change. She and Jeannie began to bond.

Then I suggested a radical idea to Jeannie. I have learned that names are very important to our animal friends, and they often ask me what their names mean. I asked if Jeannie would consider changing Misty's name to Miracle. "Misty" had a cloudy and murky connotation to it, but the name "Miracle" was clear and focused. And wasn't it a miracle that the two were mutually exploring a new beneficial friendship? Jeannie liked the suggestion; the horse did too and instantly responded to her new name.

What a prophetic name it was to be! Miracle, who has had many health problems over the years, feels it's a miracle that Jeannie has just not given up on her. For example, when Jeannie next contacted me, she seemed particularly worried. Miracle was limping badly. Jeannie asked if I would talk with Miracle, who told me, "I stepped on something awhile ago that almost sent me through the ceiling." Then Miracle sent me a picture of a thin needlelike form. She also sent me a feeling, and in one of my legs I started to experience an uncomfortable physical sensation between my ankle and shin. Soreness.

I reported to Jeannie what I had heard, seen and felt. Her confirmation about what I heard was immediate. She said; "Yes, Miracle's leg problem did start a while back, but we couldn't find anything at the time." She decided to get some x-rays. Sure enough, the x-rays revealed that several horseshoe nails had broken off and were abscessing the foot and leg area. The nails were taken out, some therapy was applied, and Miracle was romping around like a foal.

Through bad times and good, Jeannie has been there for Miracle. And Miracle has responded. Physically, emotionally and mentally, Miracle has repeatedly resonated to Jeannie's focused love. But Jeannie says that the real miracle has been her newfound ability to focus, open her heart and witness the life-affirming changes that love has brought about in Miracle.

Matthew's Melancholy

MATTHEW, A MIXED-BREED CANINE, AND KATHY, HIS human companion, adored each other. Their relationship was very close, so Kathy noticed right away when Matthew started behaving strangely. One spring morning, she called to tell me that her beloved dog had appeared to be distressed the night before and signaled repeatedly that he wanted to go outside. When Kathy and her husband let him out, however, he ran around in an agitated fashion, then came back in. That night, Matthew had climbed into bed with Kathy and her husband (a behavior he usually reserved for "dreaded" thunderstorms) and licked Kathy's hand and arm almost all night. The next morning, Matthew's health had suddenly taken a turn for the worse; even though he usually had a good appetite and activity level, he had barely left his bed or touched his food or water when Kathy called me around noon. Kathy even thought he might be dying.

After I got off the phone with Kathy, I asked Matthew what was going on. He told me he was very sad. First of all, his good friend and doggie housemate, Spot, had passed a few months before. Not only that, he said, but on the night of his strange behavior, he had seen Tobin, his littermate, who had passed some time before. Tobin had actually seemed to be waiting for him just on the other side of the sliding glass door in Kathy's living room! The two littermates had been strays together, and while Matthew had been rescued by Kathy, Tobin hadn't been so lucky. That's why Matthew had been licking Kathy's arm, as a "thank you" for not letting him perish as his brother had.

Then Matthew told me that Kathy was very sad, too. Experience has taught me that animals pick up on our emotions and thoughts with remarkable acuity, so I asked Kathy about the impression her canine friend had conveyed to me. She admitted that Matthew was telling the truth. Her father had also passed a few months ago and, as most people would be, she was still grieving. She assured me that in recent months she had made an effort to concentrate on life rather than death—but from the doleful sound of her voice, I gathered that darker thoughts might have crept in more often than she would have liked.

It was no wonder Matthew physically appeared to be dying. For several months, his good friend and caretaker had been grieving. That, coupled with the passing of his good friend, Spot, had made Matthew feel melancholy. Then, Matthew said, when Tobin appeared to him that night, "I thought Tobin was coming to get me."

I can't say if Tobin was coming for Matthew or not. I don't know why he paid that visit to his brother or what he wanted to say. What I do know is that thoughts of grief, sadness and dying seemed to pervade the household during that time. And maybe it was time for a change. Perhaps this is another way Spirit works: when we are ready to have something else presented to us, the lesson we've been searching for comes.

I decided it was important to talk some more with Kathy, and she and I began a gentle discussion. We shared our ideas about eternal life and read each other passages from some of our favorite books. At the end of our conversation, Kathy seemed refreshed and more lighthearted. So did I.

That one conversation may seem a slight thing, but I believe the consultation had such a positive effect because I just helped Kathy reaffirm what she already believed. Sometimes we just need reaffirmation in our lives to help get us back on the path. That is what I've learned about animals, and it's also true of humans. It's not like I really ever teach anybody anything, particularly when I tell animals about a Higher Force. The way I look at it is that every creature knows these Truths already. I just help to remind them.

But without Matthew's help, maybe Kathy wouldn't have realized or remembered this for some time in the future. That's why I believe our animal friends are gifts to us that Spirit puts in our path. They can reflect some of our own issues back at us, and in our efforts to help them we embrace the opportunity to look, listen, take a step back, reflect and learn the lessons necessary for us to proceed on our spiritual path.

In one week, I received a note from Kathy. Since the day of our conversation, Matthew had been up and around and playing. It appears that he instantly picked up on Kathy's fresh new perspective and was responding to it. From that day on, Kathy has been more cognizant that her thoughts can affect Matthew, so in a way, Matthew helps

Kathy keep her thoughts "in line." This has been a blessing for both of them!

I think of this story when my brain tries to wander into dark places. It is a constant reminder to me to keep my thoughts as fresh and new as that spring day when Kathy first called. Not only for myself, although that is important. I now realize that the health of my animals might depend on it.

Sam Sees His Future

FROM THE BEGINNING, I KNEW SAM WAS A DOG WITH good intentions. An even-tempered eleven-year-old, he had had a good life with a family who cared for him very much. That's why they called me. Sam had developed serious knee problems, along with some other ailments, and his guardians wanted me to ask him if he was happy, if he was hurting, and how they could make his life better.

My job often allows me to experience the same sensations the animal is feeling, and I picked up on Sam's hurting knee right away, since my own left knee began to ache.

Now, I don't want to be in pain any more than the animal does, so I decided to talk to Sam immediately.

When an animal seems to be in pain, I will often begin by asking simply, "What happened?" If there seems to be a physical "cause," animals tend to show me a picture of what happened to them just before they began to feel discomfort—for example, jumping out of a van and landing the wrong way. The human companion often asks me if they should bring the animal friend to see a veterinarian. I support and encourage them to do whatever they feel is right to help the animal in a safe and effective way. In fact, the animal friend will sometimes tell me, "I want to see someone." I have come to understand that this is their direct, actual request to see a veterinarian.

But this didn't happen in Sam's case, and I thought there might be a psychological reason for his discomfort. I have found that animals, like all spiritual beings regardless of form, can suffer from emotional and psychological pain that may manifest as physical pain. Many animals seem to benefit from being reminded that they are loved by a Higher Power who wants them to be happy and healthy. We are all valuable, I tell them, and have a *right* to health and happiness—so the time for healing an old emotion or pain is *now*.

Sam liked hearing about this loving Force, and his health seemed to improve for a while. Then, to my surprise, he took a turn for the worse. Several ailments caused him to complain, and his family eventually called me to see if Sam wanted to be euthanized.

From my experience, "euthanized" is not a word that animals are familiar with. I have learned that the vast majority of animals don't believe in a point of termination. They believe they "pass" to other, new experiences. Consequently, there is little fear about "going on." This is refreshing, delightful, and a very different view from what most humans hold.

When I asked Sam what he would like to do, he surprised me again. He said that what he would really like to do was to work as a helping animal with young children who were somehow in need of him—children whom we might call "handicapped." Sam wanted to spend time with them and make them happy.

I spoke to his family, but I sensed a reticence about allowing him to do this. I had the feeling they thought he wasn't capable of such work in his condition. Sam continued to voice his strong desire, but eventually he seemed to see that his family just did not believe he could do the work. He told me he was ready to go.

Like his sudden turn with his ailments, Sam's change in attitude puzzled me. It was many months later, when discussing the case with the person who had originally contacted me, that I learned some very interesting information. It seems there was a family member who frequently voiced her opinion that Sam should be "put down"—right in front of him! This family member's thoughts may have influenced Sam's consciousness, and even his physical condition. After all, if you have people around you who constantly tell you that you're sick, you are going to believe it! I think that is what happened to Sam. I believe that he may have picked up on this other person's thoughts, and come to accept her beliefs that he was sick and that he should "go."

Sam wanted to be of service to young children, but he sensed that the only way he was going to be able to achieve this was to "go." Therefore, I believe Sam's physical condition resulted from the change in his psychological condition. At this point, I believe Sam made the choice to "go."

Sam's case shows how very important it is to have all members of a family in concert about the feelings, wishes and messages that are sent to an animal. As can be seen in this case, our animal friends pick up on our thoughts very readily. When family members ask what they can do to give their animal friends the mental message that they want them to be healthy, I advocate taking a class in animal communication. They can learn many ways to give mental, pictorial and emotional comfort to their friends. One simple method is sending the animal friend mental pictures of himself or herself in perfect physical condition. I have learned that this not only gives the animal a model to look to, but also seems to give him or her encouragement. The best way to mentally assist our animal friends is for the humans to think thoughts of health, not of sickness. And, as always, we must appreciate that our animal friends are intelligent and have their own vision for their life and future.

Augie's Awesome Amplitude

AT ONLY TWO YEARS OLD, AUGIE, AN UNUSUALLY LARGE golden retriever, had already had an operation on one hind leg and was due for an operation on the other. Judy, his guardian, contacted me because she wanted to know if Augie was in pain. But that wasn't all she needed to know. Since her husband, Lem, had passed about a year ago, Judy hadn't been able to walk Augie around the block. Augie would just sit in the house and mope, she said. And he seemed to be afraid of lots of things. Sounds. Trucks. Even the sound of people laughing could send him pulling her back into the house.

When Augie refused to go outside, Judy stayed home with him. This impaired her efforts to begin a new social life after her husband's passing, but she was willing to do it in order to keep Augie company. But Judy was concerned for Augie's well-being. She suspected that his health problems weren't the only cause of his reluctance to leave the house. She knew there must be a psychological reason why Augie wouldn't walk with her, and why he seemed so afraid.

Judy was right. Immediately, Augie explained to me how much he missed his good friend Lem. He was still waiting for Lem to return to the house and wanted to be there to greet him when he arrived. That was one reason he didn't want to leave for walks. I explained to Augie that Lem had completed his life mission here for now and that, when it was the right time, Augie would see Lem again. I suggested to Judy that she play the classical music that Lem had loved (and Augie missed, he told me). I also suggested that Judy give Augie a piece of Lem's clothing, just for comfort. Judy did these things, and told me that she, too, began to receive comfort in hearing the familiar music and seeing some of Lem's old things. Augie appeared to be a bit happier. We were getting good results.

Judy then invited me to pay a home visit to Augie. When I entered the townhouse, I especially noticed Judy's lovely furniture. Her surroundings were done in exquisite taste—but there was furniture all around. In a townhouse, this certainly limited Augie's ability to be mobile. No wonder he just sat around! The more I talked with Judy, however, the more I realized how intuitive she was. I never mentioned the furniture, but the next week Judy called me and said she had reorganized the furniture on the first floor so that Augie could move more freely.

Then there was the issue of Augie's legs. Unknowingly, Judy had made such an issue of telling Augie and everyone around him how bad his legs were that Augie felt like an invalid. He literally didn't see how he could protect Judy if she got attacked when they were walking. That was the primary reason he didn't want to go on walks. He wouldn't be able to protect his dear friend! We settled this by having Judy carry a little billy club that fit in her hand. Every time she would try to take Augie for a walk, she would show the club to him and assure him that she could defend herself. Also, at 107 pounds, Augie was a big two-year-old. I told him he could certainly defend Judy just by being who he was—that his size was probably a deterrent to anyone who might think of harming his friend.

Augie's size was a disadvantage in one respect, though: most other dogs were afraid of him, so he didn't have any doggie playmates. I asked him if this bothered him, and he told me it made him very sad. I assured him that it was only his large size, and not his personality, that scared other dogs away from him. (I mentally showed him a picture of himself standing next to a small horse, so he could get a sense of how a smaller dog might feel standing next to him!) Augie seemed comforted by this. But while Judy fretted over Augie's lack of canine friends, I was concerned that Augie didn't have any human male friends. I suggested to Judy that perhaps she could get one of her male neighbors to befriend Augie, to help ease the pain of losing Lem.

There is something in the universe that has a way of providing what we most need. Sure enough, a male neighbor began to stop over on a regular basis and was able to take Augie for a daily walk. On top of that, a doggie playmate for Augie surfaced, and now Augie has a friend he looks forward to seeing when he walks to the park. And, because he is more active, he is losing some extra weight that was a bit hard on his legs.

Another fortunate development for Augie occurred when Judy bought a new car. Because of his legs, Augie had had a hard time getting into the old one, but this one was easier for him, so Judy could take Augie to more places with her. She could even take him to doggie day care, which he loved. Now, instead of being cooped up at home, Augie had new and exciting things to see—and Judy could get out more, too.

When I talk with Augie now, the first thing he always tells me is how much he loves Judy. He thanks her for putting up with him and his legs and is very grateful that she takes such good care of him. And Judy, in turn, feels she has a better understanding of Augie, and of herself. She has become more flexible and patient, and is very aware when Augie simply does not want to go for a walk. At these times, she doesn't force the issue. She has redone her little patio to make a place for Augie to bring his toys and lie in when he's feeling down. She and Augie are a team now, she tells him, and they must stick together and help each other.

Despite their painful loss, Augie now feels happier, and Judy feels more at ease. Augie's new peace of mind has given her the freedom to start socializing again. When she goes out, however, she remembers to tell Augie why she is going, and why she can't take him with her. Then she murmurs the three little words an animal friend most wants to hear when his or her beloved guardian leaves: "I'll be back."

Spiritual Lessons

Leonard Learns That Life Goes On

LEONARD IS AN ADORABLE FOURTEEN-YEAR-OLD ORANGE tabby who lives in a house with two other feline friends, one canine companion and a human, Amanda. Amanda called me one day in alarm because of a physical problem the tabby had developed seemingly overnight: it looked like Leonard was experiencing severe receding gum tissue in his mouth. Amanda was concerned about the speed with which the gums had seemed to deteriorate, and worried that Leonard might begin to lose his teeth.

Amanda also confided to me that Leonard had a close friend, a cat named Wesley, who had passed just the week before. Until Wesley's passing, he and Leonard had been best buddies and played together constantly. Now Leonard moped and pined, and Amanda was sure he missed Wesley. But she didn't understand how the emotional pain Leonard might be feeling could possibly have produced such a striking physical ailment. So she asked if I would talk with her feline friend to find out if he knew what was happening.

When I spoke with Leonard he said that he was literally "torn up" about losing Wesley. He was in emotional and physical pain. He felt as if he didn't have a purpose anymore, because he believed his purpose was to play with Wesley and be his friend. Because Leonard was a very nurturing cat, who had "mothered" and protected Wesley, I wondered whether having a little kitten to take care of might help him over the loss of his friend.*

---

* Many clients ask me to ask this question of their animals, and I tell them that I prefer not to ask the animal until I have their promise that they are really considering adopting another animal friend. I explain that I don't want to get the animal's hopes up only to be disappointed and advise them to wait until they've decided whether they can handle an addition to the family. Once they've made the commitment, I contact the animal. One time, when a client asked me to ask her dog if he would like another doggie companion, he replied in the affirmative—"anything but a small white dog." When I told his guardian, she was amazed and disappointed. What the family had talked about getting, and had had their heart set on, was a small white poodle. Apparently, their current doggie had picked up on their intentions very well!

I asked if he would like a kitten to befriend and play with, but Leonard said no, that wasn't really his thing. A kitten couldn't take Wesley's place, and what he wanted was to see Wesley.

Now this was a tall order. However, I have communicated with many animals over the years who have passed to a new experience. It's amazing (and wonderful!) but true. The animals tell me about the things they did with their human companions in this life (which I later verify with my clients), and about what they're doing now. I promised Leonard I would try to contact Wesley and see if Wesley would agree to visit him.*

Then Leonard asked me, "Are you absolutely certain we don't die—that we just pass to something else?" I was thrilled that I could emphatically answer "Yes!" My communications with other animals who have passed leave no doubt in my mind. It seems that animals have a large choice of things they can do when they pass. They may help in the transition of other animals who are passing, or they may just play. Some have children (they show me their kittens, cubs or pups, for example), and some stay by their humans. Some seem to come back to this reality in a different form,

* Please note that although I receive calls from guardians of animals that have passed, my primary focus is communicating with animals who are on this plane. There are other animal communicators who specialize in cases of animals who have passed.

perhaps a different breed or a different species altogether. Sometimes they come back to experience what it's like to have fur or wings, etc. "Passing" to something else seems to be a great adventure for our animal friends.

Leonard was overjoyed to hear this. He sighed in relief and told me he was quite happy that I would attempt to talk with Wesley. About a week later, Amanda called me to let me know that Leonard's loss of gum certainly seemed to be related to his having felt the loss of Wesley. Since I had spoken with Leonard, at least one tooth that had been protruding badly with little or no gum tissue now appeared normal. (To be certain, though, she took him to the vet, where he had several teeth pulled.)

Meanwhile, I had managed to contact Wesley, who lovingly agreed to visit Leonard. He was very busy doing other enjoyable things, however, and Leonard had to wait a few days! (Believe it or not, Wesley was listening to music—classical music—and he was really enjoying it. While some animals have told me that they don't enjoy classical music, Amanda, a cellist, wasn't surprised when I told her what Wesley was doing, because he had often come to sit by her when she played.) But when I last spoke with Leonard, he stated that he had definitely received a visit from Wesley. I don't know what the two cats said to each other, but I do know that the visit was healing for Leonard, because of the picture he sent me of himself. He wanted me to see that this once-mournful tabby was now curled up, happy, and sleeping as contentedly as any cat I had ever seen.

Clancy is Clear about the Creator

CLANCY WANTS HIS STORY KNOWN, AND I PROMISED I would tell people about him. He wants other people and animals to know what he endured so that if they have a rough time, they'll know that they shouldn't give up. Things can get better. That's what happened to Clancy.

Carrie, Clancy's second human companion, sensed that her horse had been abused. When she asked me to uncover what had happened to him I hesitated. This was not a case I was sure I should take. Over the years, I've learned that my days can be filled with exhilarating and blissful moments, whether I'm sharing the happiness an animal friend feels about his or her guardian or hearing human clients tell me about a "complete turnaround" in their relationship with their animal friend due to a consultation. But there are times when it is very difficult to hear the things an animal tells me. I wish I could tell you that it gets easier through the years to hear these things, but it doesn't. I try to "steel" my heart a bit when people want me to ask their animal friends what their lives were like before they met, because I never know what I will hear. In this case, Carrie had let me know beforehand that she thought Clancy had been badly abused. But she was very sincere and wanted the best possible life for Clancy. He seemed to have some strange behaviors, and she needed to know more about his background in order to help him overcome them.

After Clancy told me all that had happened to him at the hands of an alcoholic bully, I told Carrie, and we cried together. The tales of starvation and abuse explained why Clancy didn't want to be touched in certain places, and why he sucked on wood. (There are lots of different reasons horses suck on wood, but from talking with Clancy, it was apparent to me that this behavior stemmed from his background of abuse.) It also gave a bit of insight into why, now, he wasn't eating.

That was the big problem: Clancy simply wouldn't eat, and he was losing weight fast. I asked Clancy whether Carrie needed to change his feed. The feed was recently purchased, but Clancy told me it had some insects in it, which reminded him of the infested feed he'd been given in his days of hardship. Carrie replaced the feed and made sure the new feed came from a different source. But Clancy still seemed depressed, she said.

As I spoke to Clancy, I got the feeling someone was scaring him. Sure enough, Carrie verified that there were footprints in the snow in Clancy's stall that were not hers. They seemed to have been made by big shoes or boots. Was someone terrorizing Clancy?

Clancy verified that a man had been in the stall but hadn't seemed to want to hurt him. Carrie called a friend on the police force to be on the lookout and patrol the area for a while.

Carrie spent as much time as she could with Clancy, but she had a regular job and a life that kept her busy. She was also a little afraid to go to the barn, since she thought the mysterious man might be waiting for her there. Her visits to Clancy became less regular. I felt Clancy could sense the tension this new situation caused in Carrie, and he still wasn't eating very much. When I probed further, I found that Clancy was worried by the infrequency of Carrie's visits. He thought she was going to neglect him just as his first caretaker had done. Now I knew we had hit the root of the problem. Clancy feared he would be neglected again, and he was dependent, maybe too dependent, on Carrie. He felt she was his only friend. I knew what I needed to do.

I asked Carrie if I could have some time with Clancy to teach him about a loving Force, a friendly power that provides safety and can help us in loneliness. Now, I know that there are a lot of people who still don't believe that animals are sentient, heart-filled beings, but my work has shown me differently. Clancy is proof of it.

I assured Clancy that his life with Carrie would be better than it had been before. I asked if he could help her, too. I explained that if he ate, she would feel better and happier.

Then I told him that he never needed to be alone again—that his good friend Carrie wasn't his only friend. I suggested, for example, that he could make friends with the birds around his pasture and barn. Within two days, Clancy had some bird friends that would regularly land on him! I also told him that the grass was his friend and the sun was his friend, and that these were all symbols of a great and friendly Force that would be with him always. This good and loving Force, I said, was closer than his own breath.

I began to feel a change in Clancy—and he started eating. I asked Carrie if I could send down some metaphysically oriented cassette tapes for Clancy, since he was apparently quite an advanced thinker! This may sound like an odd request—after all, it's one thing to communicate with an animal personally through the mind and the heart, but you may wonder whether I really thought Clancy could benefit from hearing lectures played on a tape machine. In fact, I have learned that our animal friends can often understand words, thoughts and expressions, especially when these are accompanied by corresponding mental images a guardian can send. I will often read to the animal friends in my own household, and recommend to many of my clients that they do this, too. Some clients read passages from the Bible, or from a beloved book that speaks about love, forgiveness or joy. Carrie said she would play the lecture tapes in Clancy's barn when she couldn't be around.

I was so grateful that Carrie agreed to do this. So many people would not have. And why not? Aren't we all in this together? Why should we believe that we are spiritual beings, but that animals are not—that we can walk a spiritual path, but they cannot? Many of the great spiritual Masters have seemed to love these beings called animals. Buddha said that "when a man has pity on all living creatures, only then is he noble." Allah talks about bees being spiritual creatures and carrying divine messages to us. Jesus proclaimed, "Go into all the world and preach the gospel to every *creature*." He didn't say just your fellow human beings.

Why don't we listen? Why don't we embrace animals' divinity, too? Of course, if we believed that animals were spiritual beings, just as we are, we would have to treat them with dignity. Maybe that's what some people are afraid of.

Kelly Cultivates Completeness

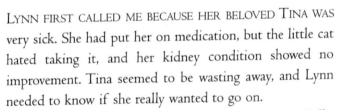

LYNN FIRST CALLED ME BECAUSE HER BELOVED TINA WAS very sick. She had put her on medication, but the little cat hated taking it, and her kidney condition showed no improvement. Tina seemed to be wasting away, and Lynn needed to know if she really wanted to go on.

Lynn also wanted me to talk to her other cat, Kelly, who had never seemed to get along with Tina. To be sure, the cats had different personalities. Lynn told me how Tina would snuggle up and sit on her lap for hours on end. She was an easy cat to love. Kelly, however, always seemed distant. Sometimes she'd rub up against a leg, but she definitely wasn't a lap cat. And she often seemed to be stalking Tina! Tina's health condition and Kelly's stalking concerned Lynn. Time to talk to Tina and Kelly.

As it turned out, it wasn't that Kelly didn't like Tina— she just wanted to teach her to be, in her words, "a better cat." Now, she wasn't talking about the kind of traits that we think might make a human "a better person." Kelly thought Tina could afford to be a little more . . . feline. Lynn, when I asked her, agreed, pointing out that Tina didn't know how to fight. Perhaps Kelly's stalking her would show her how to be quicker, more alert and better able to defend herself.

But Kelly had much more than that to teach. Indeed, both cats felt that they had specific purposes for being in Lynn's life, and they tried to behave accordingly. Tina told me she was there to be a soft kitty, to show Lynn to be soft to herself, to take care of herself, and in general, to like herself more. And despite her illness, she did want to stay with Lynn and continue helping her as much as she could. Kelly's mission, on the other hand, was to help Lynn learn that she could be strong, that she had a purpose in life. She was confident that Lynn had a spiritual purpose to fulfill, a path of service to follow.

Lynn knew she wanted to be of service to others. She had studied many different things, and had read many spiritual books. She just needed to find her niche. You may ask yourself how a cat could help a human on this quest, but after my very first consultation with the felines, Lynn's interest was piqued, and slowly but surely, as she became receptive to what her animal friends had to teach her, she began to see important changes in her life.

First, Lynn's attitude toward Kelly softened. Instead of seeing Kelly as a standoffish cat, Lynn began to appreciate her more for what she was: a teacher. As her understanding and love for Kelly began to grow, Lynn noticed that Kelly had taken to staring at her for long periods of time. Perplexed, she called to ask me what was going on. Kelly told me that Lynn was not being a very good student!— that is, she was too busy hurrying through her day to pay attention to what Kelly was trying to tell her. In short, Lynn should slow down! She decided to give Kelly's advice a try, and consciously slowed the pace of her life.

Before too long, Lynn called again, this time to ask why Kelly paced around the house, looking uncomfortable. Kelly told me that the "thump, thump, thump sounds" were annoying her, and she couldn't rest. When I described the sounds to Lynn, she immediately identified them as coming from the road construction near the house. She had actually forgotten about the construction and had no idea that the impact of the sounds could disturb Kelly so much. This was proof positive to Lynn that Kelly was communicating with me (which made her even more receptive to Kelly's messages), and an indication to me that Lynn was becoming more observant of Kelly. Slowly but surely, this feline was making Lynn a student "fit" to be taught!

Then the nonstop meowing began. When I checked in, Kelly said she was trying to let Lynn know that she recognized the importance of her human friend's dreams. Kelly believed that Lynn's dreams were very important, and advised her to start writing them down. Lynn began to record her dreams, a process that became an invaluable tool as she began to view her dreams as "things to come." She reviewed what she had written in her "dream" book and thought about the meaning of her dreams. She even took a course on increased spirituality and dreaming! Little by little, through Kelly's suggestions, Lynn opened her consciousness to whole different realms of possibilities for ways to grow. She even quit her part-time job and began to do feng shui consulting—something she loved! Her whole world was expanding, and Kelly had started the process.

Lynn and I had formed a friendship, and I could tell that she was listening more and more to *both* pussycats. She became softer when she needed to and more assertive when she needed to. The more the cats communicated with Lynn, and Lynn did what they suggested, the more confident she became about their advice. They showed their value to her, and she became happier with herself. Now, some people who read this may doubt that an animal friend could really have the capacity to work these changes in a person's life. But Kelly was very certain that she was a spiritual healer and teacher, and, while this may be a difficult concept for some to accept, the following events erased any doubt from my mind.

Lynn contacted me about a month after our first consultation and said that Kelly had gotten very sick. Now, just like Tina, Kelly had been diagnosed with kidney trouble. Lynn asked if I would talk to Kelly to see if she would put up with taking the medications she would need. (People often ask me to tell their animal friends why a certain medication is needed, and to try to convince them to take it calmly. I have had many clients, however, who instead want to know if their animal friend wants to take the medication or not. They ask me to tell the animal what can be expected to happen without the medication, but they want the animal to know he or she has a choice. I have learned that the animal friends are as capable of making this decision as any other decision. Most take the medication, some won't. It is a tough decision for the person, and for the animal friend. But I have learned that there are many clients who trust their animal friend's decision enough to abide by it. In this case, Lynn's decision to listen to Kelly's request was life changing for her, and for Kelly, too!)

Kelly was very firm, almost adamant. She did not want to take the medications. She plainly stated that she was helping Tina with her kidney problem by "taking" the pain and symptoms on herself before getting rid of them. I'll never forget what she said: "Give me two weeks. I'll be better." And she was! Lynn took Kelly back to the veterinarian after about two weeks and she was fine. In addition, Tina was eating better, looked better, and seemed all-around healthier.

But here's the best part: A few days before New Year's Eve last year, Lynn called to let me know that Kelly had been acting strange. She was more affectionate than usual, constantly brushing up against Lynn's legs. What was going on? Kelly told me, very precisely, "Tell her (Lynn) to be sober, to be lucid and to be clear. And not to go anywhere for the next several days!"

Lynn was startled and very disappointed. She and her husband had planned a trip to visit relatives in another state, and they were scheduled to leave within the next three days. But I reminded Lynn that if Kelly had been trustworthy in the past, she could trust her now. This was a big decision for Lynn. How do you tell your relatives that you're not coming because your cat told you not to? Lynn was very courageous. She decided to listen to Kelly, and to *be sober, be lucid* and *be clear.*

Well, it turns out that Kelly was right. Right at the time when Lynn and her husband would have been driving, her husband began experiencing severe arterial fibrillations. He ended up in the hospital for the rest of the holidays. But thanks to Kelly, he wasn't out on the road, where help could have taken a long time to get to him. He was at home, where medical attention was easily accessible. Kelly helped save his life.

It makes one wonder: Who is to say who teaches whom? Who is to say that only humans can help or heal? Lynn, who now knows Kelly as a "true sage and wise teacher," would say otherwise. Perhaps if we learned to look at both humans and animals as spiritual beings, we would come to see that more of us are capable of healing and teaching than we ever thought possible.

What We Do Matters

Cindy, the Cinderella Cat

IT OFTEN HAPPENS THAT INDOOR CATS WHO HAVE NEVER had the opportunity to enjoy the outdoors will run through an open door and lose their way outside. Cindy, however, had some extra motivation for her flight—her loving guardian, Peter, had recently married a lady (we'll call her Esmeralda) who was not too fond of cats. Fearing for her furniture, Esmeralda wanted to get Cindy declawed—even though Cindy had never shown the slightest interest in

Pictured above is Tootsie, another of Betty's feline friends.

scratching any of the furniture. As for declawing, Cindy wanted none of it.

This story reminds me of Cinderella not only because of Cindy's troubled home life, but because Betty, the client who told me about Cindy, really acted as her fairy god-mother! Cindy wasn't part of Betty's family; she lived with Peter and Esmeralda down the block. But when Cindy ran away from home, Betty worried about her safety, and feared the neighbors would be too skeptical to use my serv-ices. Betty liked Cindy so much that she asked if I would help her.

Ordinarily I might have refused the case. Why? Because I find it most beneficial when the animal's closest human companion calls me. In this way, the strongest heart-to-heart connection is maintained, and that connection often helps bring an animal home. I wasn't certain Betty had that close relationship with Cindy. But something told me to say yes. Having worked with Betty once before, I felt she had enough love in her heart to help bring home an army of cats!

When communicating with lost animals, I usually start off as gently as I can, asking them how they feel, how they got out, etc. Then I ask them to tell me, by pictures, thoughts or feelings, where they are. I ask them if they are inside a home. I ask them if someone picked them up. I ask them if they took a ride in a car. I might hear, intuitively, the "whoosh" of cars or smell the aroma of garlic (maybe they are near a restaurant), or see a picture of a storefront that they are in front of. The pictures the animals send me, of course, show their surroundings from *their* height and perspective. Parking meters seem immensely tall, and streetlights seem miles high—so I have to ask a lot of questions, and sometimes the lost one is not in the best state of mind to answer them. He or she is just too scared, or too confused.

Cindy's case went on for about a week. On day one, I asked Cindy to send me pictures of where she was. Cindy sent me pictures of ditches and drainage pipes. I asked Betty if there were any exposed drainage pipes or ditches in the community. She confirmed that there were. I then suggested she go to that spot and put food and water out for Cindy that night. Sure enough, the next day the food and water were gone. Although we both agreed that any animal could have partaken of these, we eagerly hoped it was Cindy.

The next day Cindy sent me pictures of the houses she saw from her hiding place. Yellow houses, white houses, with lots of flowers, and the old familiar drain pipes. Betty located the houses that Cindy had described. And she looked in the drain pipes to see if Cindy was stuck there. No sign of Cindy yet.

The fourth day Cindy was terribly thirsty and felt lethargic. Yes, Betty confirmed, the temperature had sky-rocketed that day, and Cindy might be dehydrating. Nonetheless, she kept putting food and water out.

All along I was utilizing a technique that I had used successfully with other lost animals. I pictured a large neon sign on top of Betty's house with the words: "Cindy, come here." If you are ever called to help find an animal, you may want to use this technique, too. Here's how it works for me: From the human, I get an accurate description of the house the animal friend left from. Sometimes people will send me photos of their apartment building, or house or trailer. Then I mentally envision a huge neon sign with an arrow pointing downward. The sign might say, "Cindy, home is here." I then send that image to the animal friend. It is the total picture—the house and the sign—that I believe works. The animal friend might be very far away and unable to see where the house is, but I believe they can see the sign. It's kind of like following the star of Bethlehem. I tell the animal friend I'm putting the sign on top of their home, and I tell them what it says. I ask them to follow it as best they can, and to be careful while doing so.

Betty did her best to draw Cindy's attention to her house. Since the houses in her neighborhood may have looked too similar for Cindy to differentiate easily, she put huge pots of geraniums out front and back, and lots of enticing furniture for Cindy to sit on. I pictured these to Cindy. But after five days, still no Cindy.

Day six loomed long. My whole body ached. The feeling just came on. I wasn't consciously focusing on Cindy at the time. But I knew it had to be her, because of the cases I had at the time no other animal friend had mentioned feeling achy. I was certain Cindy had gotten in a fight with other cats. She was very tired, thirsty and now beat-up. On day seven the phone rang. Betty was almost shouting for joy. Cindy had returned! Sure enough, she was a bit torn up, but other than that, she seemed to be fine.

In the week that Cindy was gone, my friend Betty talked several times to Esmeralda and discreetly stated that she was so happy Cindy hadn't been declawed. After all, she pointed out, if Cindy ran into other cats out "on the streets," she would be able to defend herself. And this proved to be true when Cindy got in the tussle.

When Cindy returned home, Esmeralda seemed to have had a change of heart, and she and Peter were both quite happy to see her. The last time I spoke to Betty, she said that Cindy still had all her claws. So in the end, even though both Cinderella and Cindy went through some rough experiences, they both kept their good natures and essences intact. Cinderella got to keep her precious glass slippers, and Cindy got to keep her claws. And in both stories, some human hearts were softened. I'd say that's a pretty happy ending.

Charlie the Chipper Chipmunk

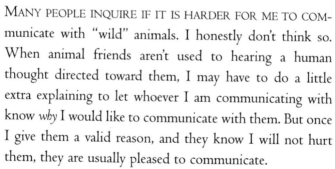

MANY PEOPLE INQUIRE IF IT IS HARDER FOR ME TO COM-
municate with "wild" animals. I honestly don't think so.
When animal friends aren't used to hearing a human
thought directed toward them, I may have to do a little
extra explaining to let whoever I am communicating with
know *why* I would like to communicate with them. But once
I give them a valid reason, and they know I will not hurt
them, they are usually pleased to communicate.

When she found a "wild" creature in need, my friend
Pamela didn't hesitate to ask me for help. "He's just a little

guy, but I get the feeling he wants to live," said Pamela. She was talking about the handsome creature who was to be named Charlie, a chipmunk who, to all appearances, could barely walk. Pamela found the little guy in the yard and brought him into her house, fed him and took care of him.

I've spoken to Charlie about six or seven times now, so I know he's a very likeable fellow. His right back leg was damaged in a fall, but he never complains, and he's not at all angry about what happened to him. While his leg mends, Pamela and her family have fed him, prayed for him and encouraged him to be whole. Though Charlie's case looked bad at first, his hosts never let up on their prayers for him, and he improves day by day. First he crawled, then his leg began moving, then he started to scurry around and hold himself—well—the way chipmunks do.

But Pamela wanted to know whether there was anything else she should be doing for Charlie. When I spoke with him, he wanted Pamela to know that she was doing a lot of important things right. He was so thankful that she keeps her five cats away from him ("They are so big!" he said), and he loves the fruits and seeds they feed him. He also appreciates that, when the family handles him, they do so carefully and gently.

There were a few more things, though, that Charlie felt he needed to make a full recovery. He told me he needed his bowl of clean water back in the glass aquarium Pamela had given him to live in. "But we've done that, and he just fills it up with wood chips!" Pamela declared, exasperated. Nonetheless, a bowl went back into the aquarium. I asked Charlie why he put the wood chips in his bowl, and he said, "I have nothing else to do!" That's when it hit me that Charlie might be bored. I asked him if he would like to go outside to breathe some fresh air, and he got very excited. He said he would love to go outside! So Pamela and her husband carefully moved his aquarium to the backyard and let him get some fresh air. (They sat outside with him so that no larger neighborhood creatures could come near and frighten him.) He enjoyed that so much that now he gets regular time on the family's screened-in porch.

The family noticed right away that Charlie's demeanor became much more active and lively when he was brought outside or allowed to run around on the porch. Before long, he was scampering around the porch so nimbly that Pamela asked me to ask him whether he felt he could go out on his own. I asked Charlie, but he answered, "Not yet." Didn't he mind living with the family? Pamela wondered. "I like it here!" Charlie declared happily. "When I'm ready to go, I'll let them know." And I bet he will. Our animal friends have a way of communicating with us. Sometimes if we really concentrate, we will get a thought or "feeling" from them, and then we just know. And I am certain that Pamela and her family will continue praying and giving the little fellow good support, until that fine day finally comes.

In the meantime, Charlie is grateful. Every time he talks with me, he's so happy that Pamela and her family took him in. The animals I have spoken with always know when they have been rescued. They tell me they "wouldn't be here" if it weren't for someone finding them or taking them in. Many animals who come from shelters refer to the person who comes and takes them home as a "savior." Other animals will not let me end the consultation until they have told me how grateful they are to have been rescued by their new guardian—and they insist that I tell this to their person. For some, it is the most important thing they want to say in the whole consultation. When we help to save an animal's life, he or she never forgets. And when Charlie does strike out on his own, he told me, he won't go far. Sending me a picture of Pamela's house and yard, he said, "I have everything I want right here."

Tiffany and the Terrible Tumble

WHEN I GOT THE TELEPHONE CALL, THE FIRST THING I wondered was whether Tiffany the cat had jumped from the balcony where her "dad," Michael, had let her out to get some fresh air, or whether her three-story fall was just an accident. But Tiffany assured me she hadn't jumped from the balcony. The night she fell, she was peering near the edge and was swept off by a gust of late fall wind. Now, however, the picture didn't look too good. Tiffany told me she was in great pain—physical pain, yes, but even greater emotional pain.

Tiffany worried night and day about Michael. He had brought her from an Indiana farm to the big city of Chicago about three months before. He had just gotten divorced—a third time. He was lonely. He was looking for a job. And he didn't have a lot of money. Sadly, that was the "practical" reason I was getting this call. Should Michael euthanize Tiffany or spend the money to "fix her up?" Did she want to go?

I needed to know more. Some animal friends need to talk for a while before they open up to let me know that they are concerned or worried about something. When we reach that part of the process, I take extra note, because they are usually revealing something that is deeply felt. I asked Tiffany if she was worried just about Michael, or if she was fearful and worried about something else.

Maybe it was the condition she was in, but Tiffany opened up to me quickly. She told me that she had just come from living on the beautiful farm, where there had been lots of places for her to roam, to hide or to sit lazily in the sun. Now she was kept indoors in a one-bedroom apartment with no lovely view. And it was chilly. While Michael hunted for jobs, Tiffany was too cold to hunt for mice in the apartment. She simply stayed by a radiator and curled up trying to keep warm while her best friend, Michael, was away. And it seemed to her that he was away all the time.

I got the feeling that Tiffany really needed things to change. She wanted to stay in order to be with Michael, but I think she needed some assurance that things would be different for her in the future. She asked if she would ever go back to the farm she had loved. She asked if she would ever be warm inside again. She asked if Michael would be home more. She asked if she would ever feel better again.

I sometimes find this last question difficult to answer for the animals. But here's how I do it. If they have to go through an operation, I explain why the guardian feels it's needed. I let them know that the guardian has done everything he or she can to make sure they will feel comfortable. I let them know what the veterinarian has said—for example, that they are expected to have full recovery of their legs, or that they should be able to run again, or that they may not limp anymore, or that their mouth will feel better, etc. If the guardian doesn't know what the prognosis is, I often ask him or her to go back to the veterinarian and find out this information. I think that is the fairest way to give the information to the animal friend. And I've never had a human client who wasn't willing to do this.

In Tiffany's case, the question had to be decided quickly, so when she asked me if she would ever feel better again, I assured her that when pussycats had problems like she did, they usually felt better after an operation. Then I asked her whether she wanted to have the operation and stay with Michael. She responded immediately and emphatically: "Yes! I want to be near him, I want him to love me. I want to stay with him!"

Well, that settled that. Somehow Michael scraped together the $1,500 for the vet bill, and it wasn't too long before Tiffany fully recovered.

This experience was not pleasant for Tiffany or Michael, but I believe their bond became even stronger because of it. Michael tried to make the new apartment more homelike for Tiffany, with some new toys and a nice plush rug. A new friend of his brought Tiffany the occasional can of tuna. Tiffany even found a nice sunny spot to sit in once the fall sun had shifted—right on top of Michael's computer.

Michael eventually got a job selling real estate, and his work keeps him away from home for more hours than Tiffany likes. But she knows that he's out making "tuna" money so she can eat in style. And she knows now how important she is to him. While three wives have come and gone, Tiffany and Michael have maintained a close relationship in which both benefit from giving and receiving love. Perhaps this human and feline couple actually understand each other better than some human couples do!

Ben the Benevolent Bull

THE TOWN MEETING WAS TURNING UGLY WITH AN UNSET-tling undercurrent of frustration and outrage. Farmers, teachers and neighbors were arguing, pleading or making speeches. The one thing that had been made clear, however, was that Ben the bull was being sentenced to death.

Ben's longtime residence was a farm that had recently been sold. It had been purchased with an agreement that the property would become a demonstration farm. Now it was said that Ben, the only bull on the farm, posed a potential danger to the visiting public. It was feared that Ben might become more ornery as he aged. Several committee members thought he might attack visitors or were afraid that small children would somehow climb into his pen. In addition, officials claimed that he was an old bull, probably couldn't sire any more calves and so had outlived his usefulness on the farm. Although he had never hurt anyone on the farm before and was considered gentle by those who had worked around him, Ben would be sold at auction.

In the audience that night, one woman in particular decided to act on Ben's behalf. Ruth is a woman just like you and me, who lives in the area and had read about Ben's plight in the local paper. She feels strongly about animals and their rights and was incensed about the possibility of Ben's demise. So she passed out leaflets. She called her friends. She called the media. She made the public aware that the tax dollars they had voted to use to buy the farm might be used to kill the farm's innocent bull.

Many members of the public responded. Adults and children from both in and out of town wrote letters to the town officials, and the media reported several meetings' discussions. I too had attended the meetings and followed the issue closely, so when I was asked by Ruth to talk with Ben, I was delighted. I wasn't prepared, however, to find an animal who was so in tune with human fears and the limitations of human thought.

During our first conversation, Ben let me know that he was extremely confused. He couldn't understand why all of a sudden people wanted him slaughtered. I explained the changes that were taking place on the farm. Mostly I let him know that there were many humans who wanted him to live; he had many friends.

I vowed that I would keep him posted on what happened during the meetings. At each meeting, animal advocates debated with people who had been educated to think of Ben as simply a farm animal, a creature put here on the earth primarily to fulfill human needs. Many passionate speeches were given by both sides. Then the town officials made the announcement: an alternative had been found. Ben the bull would be moved to a farm sanctuary to live out the rest of his life in peace. I was elated and rushed up to Ruth to hug her. I couldn't wait to tell Ben that Ruth and the other advocates had helped save his life! And then came the condition. The sanctuary would take him . . . but first he had to be castrated.

There were several reasons for this. The sanctuary had many older and infirm cattle, and if Ben mounted these animals, it could cause a problem. The sanctuary also wanted to help Ben become more social. They decided that neutering would help him be less aggressive toward other animals. They wanted Ben to experience life to the fullest.

They didn't want to have to separate him from the other animals in the sanctuary. They wanted him to be able to roam in the pasture and mingle.

Ruth arranged for Ben to travel in style: a sleek, air-conditioned trailer with an attendant. He would travel to a university with a veterinary school, where the operation would be performed. Afterwards, he would be transported to the sanctuary.

Ruth wanted me to explain all this to Ben, but I found it wasn't easy. When I showed Ben that he would have to be castrated, he couldn't believe it! To quote, "You mean that in order to live, I have to have my b——s cut off?"

It depends upon the situation, but often I explain to animal friends that spaying and neutering help to solve the problem of homeless animals. When I do this, the animals usually accept the idea. In this case, even I was astonished at Ben's all-too-clear grasp of the situation. The people at the sanctuary were doing their best to help Ben. They had made a commitment to care for him with kindness for the rest of his days. But I felt ashamed he had been put in this position, ashamed that this was the best we could offer him. At that moment I felt ashamed to be human.

And so I apologized. I apologized for the whole human race. In my heart, I apologized to all the animals who have ever had their options limited, who have had no voice or have been discarded.

I couldn't help myself. I broke down and sobbed. The unfairness of Ben's predicament seemed to hit me all at once, with a one-two-three bull's eye punch. And maybe that's how he meant for his comment to feel. But I don't think so, because just at that moment he thanked me. He thanked me for taking the time to talk to him and explain what was happening.

And he was grateful to those who had intervened to save his life. I specifically told him about Ruth, who had done so much for him. I told him what she looked like, too, since despite all her efforts on his behalf, the two had never met. Ben said he would never forget her kindness. I had no idea that he would take action to express his gratitude himself!

The day of the move came, and Ben was being led from his stall into the trailer by a handler. No one was allowed by the vehicle, but Ruth boldly stepped beside the trailer's sliding glass window. All of a sudden, Ben shoved open the window with his nose and stuck his head out, not even twelve inches from Ruth. They finally met face to face.

Ruth said she stood in awe, looking into his eyes, feeling his gratitude and gentleness. Then the trailer pulled away.

Ben loves his new caretakers, and they love him. He has a large stall, and he can roam and visit cows, munch and rest to his heart's content. Residents of the community come by to meet and greet him. And when Ruth made the five-hour drive to visit her friend, she could tell him that he would be safe from now on. She told me, "What a tremendous visit I had—I walked up to Ben and re-introduced myself. He looked away from what he was doing and stretched out his neck to look at me, with his head cocked to get a good look. I again told him 'I'm Ruth,' and he nodded his head to affirm that he understood that. When I left, he was contentedly chewing hay."

I was privileged to get to know this benevolent bull, but more than communication with Ben was needed to bring his story to a happy ending. Ruth isn't an animal communicator, but that didn't stop her from helping Ben. Any of us can get involved in helping animals in our apartment building, condo, neighborhood and community. In this case, thanks to the efforts of Ruth and others to get their voices heard, the town officials *listened* and came up with a solution. It was truly democracy in action, and Ben is living proof: when we speak up for the animals, we really can make a difference.

Ruby the Rescue Dog

I WORK WITH A LOT OF RESCUE DOGS—DOGS WHO HAVE come from shelters or adoption groups or have been "rescued" from sad conditions. Ruby was a thirteen-year-old rescue dog I will never forget—not because she had had a rough early life, but because of the newborn love she found in her rescuers' home . . . when it was almost too late.

I was contacted by Brenda, the "mom" of the house, who asked me to do a home visit. When I entered their condo, I noticed that Ruby didn't come to the door. This

Clover, a rescue dog like Ruby, sleeps soundly in her hooded sweatshirt.

was unusual, because most doggies are happy to greet me. Brenda explained that Ruby was with her son, Christopher, in his bedroom. Ruby was really his dog, but as Brenda saw it, that was part of the problem. First, though, she explained the family's most pressing question. Ruby was really ill and needed an operation that would remove several tumors. She had had operations before and survived, but the dog now seemed so unhappy and despondent that Brenda wanted to know whether they should "put her through it again."

She called for Christopher to come down, but instead a shouting match occurred between mother and son. Christopher thought that having an animal communicator come to the house was ridiculous. Besides, it was imposing on his sleep time. He clearly didn't want to come down to the living room, and indicated that as far as he was concerned, Ruby was doing just fine. Brenda went upstairs to talk with her son, and about ten minutes later Christopher and Ruby both joined us in the living room. Ruby lay at Brenda's feet, and Christopher sat with his arms folded, rolling his eyes as his mother talked.

From Brenda's story, I wondered if Ruby had been "rescued" by the wrong people. She had been given to Christopher as a present, and for a while the two had had a close and wonderful relationship, until Christopher developed other priorities. Brenda noticed that some of Ruby's health problems started about this time. Then Brenda confessed the issue that was most disturbing to her: more than once she had caught her son grabbing one of Ruby's baseball-sized stomach tumors in a way that she thought must be painful to Ruby. Brenda wanted to know if I could stop her son from doing this.

This was an unusual request, to say the least. I don't do house visits in order to yell at people, and I made that clear to Brenda. But suddenly, intuitively, I knew what to do. I just started to communicate with Ruby in a gentle fashion. Here's what I found out: Yes, Christopher did hurt her when he touched her sore stomach. But she wanted both Christopher and Brenda to know that she loved them very much. She felt very alone now that Christopher didn't spend any time with her, and she longed to explore areas other than the two blocks Brenda took her on for walks. She wanted to taste ice cream. She dreamed about going in the car for rides like she had done when Christopher and Brenda first brought her to their home. She said she was "so sorry" that her family had to spend money on her other operations, but that if they had the money, she would try another operation so she could remain with them a little longer.

I told her family this, and then I waited for their reaction. Brenda appreciated what Ruby had told them, but I wasn't sure about Christopher, who continued to sit with his arms folded. He seemed determined not to show any reaction to what he had just heard. Finally, in an effort to get some idea from him about his intentions toward Ruby, I asked him if he would be willing to spend one minute per day with her. Just one minute for just the two of them. Could he promise Ruby right then and there that he would spend the minute a day with her? He was silent. Then he unfolded his arms, and said, "Yes."

On that one word, Christopher's voice cracked. He was on the verge of crying. The consultation time was up, and it was time for me to go. Inwardly, I hoped the consultation had made a difference. I thanked everyone involved, and as Brenda walked me to my car, I implored her to keep in touch. But I had no word from Brenda for many months, and eventually I concluded that I would never hear from her again.

Two years later, when I was giving a night workshop on animal communication for a local high school's continuing education program, I thought I recognized Brenda in the group. She sat through the workshop without participating in any of the exercises, but just before she walked out the door she came up to me and asked if I knew who she was.

I certainly did. When I asked her how her son was, her eyes grew saucer-like. "You remember!" she exclaimed.

Brenda told me enthusiastically that after the home visit, things had changed dramatically. Christopher didn't spend just one minute per day with Ruby; he spent an hour a day with her! They took her in the car everywhere they went. She ate ice cream, and went on long walks in new neighborhoods. She became happy again. Her tumors turned out to be inoperable, and Ruby had only nine months left with Brenda and Christopher, but Brenda wanted me to know how Ruby's life had changed for the better. Then she walked out the door.

When everyone left the lecture room, I sat for a while and let myself experience the overwhelming feelings of joy and gratitude that my brief conversation with Brenda had given me. She had made an effort to follow up with me. I don't always know when or how my work will make a difference, but I have to hold onto my faith that it does.

If only we all knew what a special opportunity we have with our animal friends. They usually ask for so little, and as with Ruby, little things can make a huge difference. Let's face it, most humans lead lives filled with stimulation. But most of our animal friends' lives are small. A change that is so easy for us can make their lives—or the remainder of their lives—worth living.

To Readers of
Ask the Animals

YOU AS A CONSUMER HAVE POWER. YOU EXERCISE YOUR power every time you purchase something. So please remember to purchase only animal-friendly products. Please don't purchase products from manufacturers who continue to experiment on animals. You can often find out whether a product is cruelty-free by looking at the label, or you can contact an organization such as People for the Ethical Treatment of Animals.

And for women who are at "that" age when hormone replacement therapy may be contemplated, please, if you decide to use something, consider using a plant-based product. Although the figures change from time to time, Premarin is often cited as being the number two drug bought by women in the United States. I wonder how many of these women know of the horrendous conditions pregnant mares are subjected to so that Premarin can be manufactured. If women really knew about the animal abuse that goes into producing this drug, most would try their very best to choose an alternative.

Please wear clothes that do not cause suffering. The pain and degradation animals suffer in breeder farms and hunting traps is unfathomable. And the cruelty goes beyond fur—many people are unaware that our animal friends also suffer in the production of leather, wool, down and silk.

Please spay and neuter your animal friends. Unfortunately, there are not enough loving homes for all the animals who need them; and I have heard from the animals themsleves about the hunger and health problems they faced when they were homeless.

Lastly, if you are not a vegetarian, please consider becoming one, even for a day or two per week. By removing all meat (including poultry and fish) from your diet, you will save, on average, eighty-three animal lives per year! There are many vegetarian and vegan products that make it easy for people to eat a delicious, healthy, compassionate diet. All creatures are precious. If you truly love animals, if you befriend them and respect them, please make choices that will benefit them.

Your Best Friend

A song from the animals to us

When you feel so sad and lonely
And you feel like you can't touch the sky
Then my love is always with you
You can always know that I

Will hold you like a mother
I'll enfold you in my heart
I'll be there when you need me
We will never, ever part.

'Cause that's what I'm here for
To be your best friend.
With a heart full of love for
You that will never end.

When you feel there is no safety
In the world outside your door
And you need a little comfort
You can count on my love for

A sure and perfect love that
Will last eternally.
Just call and I will be there
You can always count on me.

'Cause that's what I'm here for
To be your best friend.
With a heart full of love for
You that will never end.

Interlude

If you feel your eyes are aching
For the love you cannot see
And you hear your heart a' breaking
Just let me know. I'll be
Your family and your good friend
Your love and company
I'll wrap my heart around you
And hold you tenderly.

'Cause that's what I'm here for
To be your best friend.
With a heart full of love for
You that will never end.
That will never, ever end.

Suggested Reading for Enjoyment and Further Understanding of the Animal Communication Process

Black Elk, W. and W.S. Lyon. *Black Elk: The Sacred Ways of a Lakota*. New York: HarperCollins, 1990.

Boone, J.A. *Kinship with All Life*. New York: Harper and Row, 1954.

Fitzpatrick, Sonya. *What the Animals Tell Me*. New York: Hyperion, 1997.

Meyers, Arthur. *Communicating with Animals, the Spiritual Connection between People and Animals*. Chicago: Contemporary Books, 1997.

Schul, Bill D. *Animal Immortality*. New York: Carroll & Graf Publishers, Inc., 1990.

Sheldrake, Rupert. *Dogs That Know When Their Owners Are Coming Home*. New York: Three Rivers Press, 1999.

Smith, Penelope. *Animal Talk*. Point Reyes Station, California: Pegasus Publications, 1989.

Zukav, Gary. *The Dancing Wu Li Masters: An Overview of the New Physics*. New York: Bantam Books, 1980.

Some Organizations That Are Working to Make a Difference

ALTHOUGH THIS LIST IS FAR FROM EXHAUSTIVE, AND I encourage you to investigate any organization to which you donate money or time, I have found the following groups, which are all working to preserve the dignity of animals or the Earth, to be worthy of attention and consideration. It goes without saying that your local animal shelters and animal rescue groups are deserving of all the help you can give.

Alaska Wildlife Alliance
P.O. Box 202022
Anchorage, AK 99520
(907) 277-0897
www.akwildlife.org

American Anti-Vivisection Society
801 Old York Road,
Ste. 204
Jenkintown, PA 19046
(800) SAY-AAVS
(800) 729-2287
www.aavs.org

American Society for the Prevention of Cruelty to Animals
424 East 92nd Street
New York, NY 10128
(212) 876-7700
www.aspca.org

American Tortoise Rescue
23852 Pacific Coast Highway, #928
Malibu, CA 90265
(800) 938-3553
www.tortoise.com

Animal Rescue and Farm Sanctuary*
P.O. Box 95
Trego, WI 54888
(715) 466-4110
www.arfs.org

Home of Ben the Bull

Bat Conservation International
P.O. Box 162603
Austin, TX 78716
(512) 327-9721
www.batcon.org

Best Friends Animal Sanctuary
5001 Angel Canyon Drive
Kanab, UT 84741
(435) 644-2001
www.bestfriends.org

Compassion Over Killing
P.O. Box 9773
Washington, DC 20016
(301) 891-2458
www.COK.net

EarthSave International
1509 Seabright Avenue, Suite B1
Santa Cruz, CA 95062
(800) 362-3648
www.earthsave.org

The Elephant Sanctuary in Hohenwald
P.O. Box 393
Hohenwald, TN 38462
(931) 796-6500
www.elephants.com

Farm Sanctuary East
P.O. Box 150
Watkins Glen, NY 14891
(607) 583-2225
www.farmsanctuary.org

Farm Sanctuary West
P.O. Box 1065
Orland, CA 95963
(530) 865-4617
www.farmsanctuary.org

The Gorilla Foundation
Box 620-640
Woodside, NC 94062
(650) ME-GO-APE
(650) 851-8504
www.gorilla.org

Havilah Farm (for retired horses)
10748 W. Dublin Road
Pearl City, IL 61062
(815) 443-2645

The Humane Society of the United States
2100 L Street NW
Washington, D.C. 20037
(202) 452-1100
www.hsus.org

International Wolf Center
1396 Highway 169
Ely, MN 55731
(218) 365-4675
www.wolf.org

Last Chance for Animals
8033 Sunset Boulevard #835
Los Angeles, CA 90046
(310) 271-6096
www.lcanimal.org

National Opossum Society
P.O. Box 21197
Catonsville, MD 21228
www.opossum.org

New Leash on Life
16742 Placerita Canyon Road
Newhall, CA 91321
(661) 255-0097
www.newleash.org

The Pacific Whale Foundation
300 Maalaea Road
Wailuku, HI 96793
(808) 249-8977
www.pacificwhale.org/index.htm.

People for the Ethical Treatment of Animals
501 Front Street
Norfolk, VA 23510
(757) 622-PETA
(757) 622-7382
www.peta.org

Primarily Primates, Incorporated
P.O. Box 207
San Antonio, TX 78291
(830) 755-4616
www.primarilyprimates.org

Redwings Horse Sanctuary
P.O. Box 58
Lockwood, CA 93932
(831) 386-0135
www.redwings.org

Riddles Elephant and Wildlife Sanctuary
233 Pumpkin Center Circle
Quitman, AR 72131
(501) 589-3291
www.elephantsanctuary.org

Sea Shepherd, International
22774 Pacific Coast Hwy
Malibu, CA 90265
(310) 456-1141
www.seashepherd.org

**Supporting and Promoting Ethics
for the Animal Kingdom**
(a humane education speakers' bureau)
5012 S. Washtenaw
Chicago, IL 60632
(773) 925-8227

Turtle Hospital
(Hidden Harbor Marine Environmental Project, Inc.)
Funded by the Hidden Harbor Motel
2396 Overseas Highway
Marathon, FL 33050
(305) 743-5376
www.turtlehospital.org

The Vital Ground Foundation
(Preserving Habitat for Grizzly Bears)
Post Office Box 982003
Park City, UT 84098
(435) 658-0009
www.vitalground.org

Wolfsong Ranch Foundation
P.O. Box 138
Rodeo, NM 88056
(505) 557-2354
http://www.biopark.org/wolf/wolfsong.htm

World Society for the Protection of Animals
34 Deloss Street
Framingham, MA 01702
(800) 883-WSPA
www.wspa-americas.org

Also Available

The Laurel Canyon Animal Company and Kim Ogden-Avrutik, Dr.P.H., intuitive animal communicator, have worked together to create music dogs want to hear!

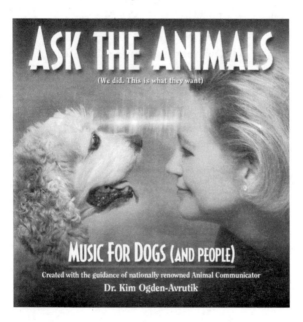

Our research involved 200 canines who were queried as to their preferences in lyrical content and music type. This population represented canines of both sexes, many ages and varied breeds from across the U.S. and Canada. Topics were taken from Dr. Kim's notebooks. All song lyrics were reviewed and edited by Dr. Kim for content and feasibility of mental and emotional comfort to the dog.

After the first tracks were recorded, Dr. Kim played them for canine focus groups. Comments from the dogs were recorded in detail and the songs were adjusted accordingly.

This is the first ever qualitatively and quantitatively researched CD based upon the preferences of hundreds of dogs!

For further information on the Ask the Animals musical CD for dogs please go to **www.petcds.com** or call **1-800-233-2880**.